TEST DRIVE

Introducing the ALERT PROGRAM® Through Song

Published by
TherapyWorks, Inc.
Albuquerque, NM
877.897.3478
www.AlertProgram.com

By
Mary Sue Williams, OTR/L
Sherry Shellenberger, OTR/L

First Printing: 2006
Second Printing: May 2008

PLEASE NOTE:

We, the authors, believe strongly that this entire book and accompanying CD empower users with the knowledge of how to help their students. We want users to be informed fully by having sufficient information and background for optimal success with the Alert Program®. Accordingly, we believe that sharing only parts of the book or CD with others who want to learn about the Alert Program® does not serve our ultimate goal in producing this publication. Copying parts of the book or CD not only violates copyright law but also compromises the benefits of the Alert Program®.

To report illegal copying of this copyrighted material, call our toll-free number at 1-877-897-3478 or go to our website to "contact us" at www.AlertProgram.com.

For those sharing the Alert Program® through in-service trainings or workshops, innovative program development, song writing, or considering the inclusion of Alert Program® information in a publication, contact TherapyWorks to receive our copyright and trademark packet. This packet provides detailed guidelines for how to use our materials. Thank you!

ISBN 0-9643041-3-9

About the Authors

In June 2003 the American Occupational Therapy Association recognized Mary Sue Williams' and Sherry Shellenberger's contributions by honoring them with the "Excellence in Intervention, Development, and Dissemination" Award.

As co-owners of TherapyWorks, Inc., Mary Sue and Sherry continue to publish products related to self-regulation. Since 1991, thousands of professionals have attended Alert Program® trainings with enthusiastic reviews. In 1996, the authors decided to lecture full-time to spread the word about using the engine analogy and how understanding self-regulation can enrich the lives of children. Since children are their finest teachers, Sherry and Mary Sue now enjoy volunteering time in the Albuquerque community where they look forward to learning more from their excellent student "instructors."

Mary Sue and Sherry have over 25 years of experience working with and learning from a variety of children, parents, and teachers in urban and rural school districts as well as clinic, home, and camp settings. They have focused on developing practical ways to teach people of all ages how to incorporate sensory integration theory into every day living. For the past two decades, they have developed, refined, and kid-tested the Alert Program. One of the authors' greatest joys is watching children find the answers to the question, "How Does Your Engine Run?"

If we are to have real peace, we must begin with the children.

Mahatma Gandhi

Acknowledgements
and Thank Yous

We cannot say enough about the wonderful people in our lives who brighten our days and lighten our hearts. We deeply appreciate all those who have offered their time and energy to help this project become a reality: our editor, graphic designer, illustrator, reviewers and "kid-testers," along with the friends and family who offered words of encouragement and their support, when we needed it most. Life is sweeter with you in our lives. Many thanks to you all.

Editor: Betsy Noll
Graphic Designer: Melissa Kostic
Illustrator: Randy Wall

Janet Auger-Bostrom
Sharon Azar
George Bach
Joanne Bach
George Bednarczyk
Kristy Boblitt
Pat Boehm
Kay Chisholm
Marsha Congdon
Julie Cook
Angelique Cook-
   Lowry
Steven Cool
Elise Dirkse
Jane Einhorn
Jada Evans
Eve Flink
Anna Garden

Jennifer Gardner
Caitlin Garder
Martha Gomez
Sandey Guidice
Ryan Guidice
Mary Hooper
L. Dennis Higgins
Molly Kaliher
Christy Kennedy
Aubrey Landes
Marci Laurel
Concepcion Lopez-
   Cherry
Lee Lyon
Andrea Maddaleni
Molly McEwen
Patti Oetter
Dick Orr

Barbara Piper
Cindy Rodenbaugh
Ed Shellenberger
Ed Shellenberger III
Cindy Shellenberger
Gabe Tovar
Delia Trapuzzano
Don Weirman
Marci Whitman
Julie Wilbarger
Carla Cay Williams
Dorothy Williams
Jay Williams
Norina Williams
Melissa Winkle
Ron Winkle
Bob Wiz
Kris Worrell

Also by the Authors

The following are existing Alert Program® publications with their official titles in italics. The abbreviated titles that will be used throughout this book are in parenthesis and a short description follows. We hope that will assist you in reading and understanding this book without the distraction of lengthy titles each time the publications are mentioned. You can visit our website for additional information on our Alert Program products and conferences at www.AlertProgram.com.

"How Does Your Engine Run?"® A Leader's Guide to the Alert Program® for Self-Regulation (**Leader's Guide**): explains the Alert Program in its entirety by guiding you through the twelve steps to teach independent self-regulation. All worksheets, charts, and pictures needed for the program are included in the 56 page Appendix section with permission to copy for educational use. Many therapists, teachers and parents have taught themselves how to use the program, just by reading the *Leader's Guide.*

An Introduction to "How Does Your Engine Run?"® The Alert Program® for Self-Regulation (**Introductory Booklet**): provides an overview of the underlying theory and key concepts of the Alert Program in an easy-to-read fashion. Share this baseline of information with other adults who want to support students who are learning about their engines and self-regulation.

Take Five! Staying Alert at Home and School (**Take Five**): was written for parents and teachers, providing activities that are helpful to support optimal states of alertness at home and school. Many therapists recommend these low budget, easy to use activities. This book does not teach children about their engine levels, but activity suggestions are organized around the five ways to change how alert one feels.

The Alert Program with Songs for Self-Regulation CD (**Songs for Self-Regulation CD**): is a double CD set. One of the CD's is an introduction to the program with excerpts from the *Introductory Booklet* read by the authors. Rather than reading the booklet, many prefer listening to this information. The second CD has fun, playful songs that help children change their engine speeds. All songs are coded so the listener will know whether they help to alert, calm or both alert and calm the nervous system.

Alert: Go Fish! and Alert Bingo (**printable games**): are card games available from our website (www.AlertProgram.com) that you can print right to your own printer. It doesn't get any easier than that! These outstanding Go Fish and Bingo game variations are sure to be favorites among children. The colorful and playful illustrations teach children the basics of the Alert Program. *Alert: Go Fish!* teaches children how to identify their levels of alertness as described in Stage One of the *Leader's Guide* by looking at cards with pictures of animals such as a lethargic beaver attempting to brush his teeth. *Alert Bingo* teaches children the five ways to change engine levels (as described in Stage Two of the *Leader's Guide*) by sorting picture tokens under the headings "Mouth, Move, Touch, Look, or Listen," rather than the traditional headings of B-I-N-G-O. Learn how quickly you can teach the Alert Program's self-regulation concepts when using these engaging games.

"How Does Your Engine Run?"® Alert Program® Conferences (**Alert Program trainings**): Meet and talk with the authors at one of their refreshing conferences and re-energize your engine. Learn why so many participants, after two days of knowledge, laughter, and practical hands-on learning, leave saying, "This is the best conference I've ever attended!"

Table of Contents

Introduction

Part **1** **one**

Introduction

The idea to write *Test Drive: Introducing the Alert Program®
Through Song* came about in a most unusual way. Sherry
Shellenberger and I (Mary Sue Williams) were sitting in our
local recording studio working on the **Just Right Song**.
As I was listening to our musician friend and colleague,
L. Dennis Higgins, EdD, play his guitar track for the song,
my thoughts wandered a bit. I started thinking about all
the ways that folks have learned about the Alert Program.
Some have learned about all the steps and stages in the
Leader's Guide (Williams & Shellenberger, 1996). Some have
read about the Alert Program theory in the *Introductory
Booklet* (Williams & Shellenberger, 1992). Others have
suggested activities and strategies to children after
reading *Take Five* (Williams & Shellenberger, 2001). Still
others have attended an Alert Program training, where
they learned how to choose which parts of the program
would best meet their children's needs. Hearing Dennis'
guitar chords in the background, I kept daydreaming
about how busy all of our lives are and thought, "Wouldn't
it be great to have a simpler, faster way to 'test drive' the
Alert Program to see if it's a match for students?"

Then as I continued listening to Dennis play his guitar,
humming along, with the **Just Right Song's** lyrics going
through my head, I thought, "This one song sums up the
Alert Program beautifully. It could almost stand alone as
a single CD. Maybe it could be the simplest, fastest way
to teach the Alert Program to students, if one were really
short on time." I leaned over to Sherry and whispered the
idea to her, so as to not interrupt Dennis' concentration.
We both beamed when we realized that, with a book to

SIDE NOTE:

*Talking about
"engines" has become
commonplace in many
schools and homes as
a way to describe how
alert one feels, whether
in high (frenzied), low
(sluggish), or just right
(alert and focused) gears.
In 1987, Mary Sue first
used the engine analogy
as a way to meet one
child's need to learn
self-regulation. Together
with Sherry and the many
clients that followed
over the decades, the
Alert Program's simple,
yet practical approach
grew in popularity, even
around the world. The
engine terminology seems
to be readily understood
by most children and their
adults, quickly becoming
a shared language to
discuss what we all do
to regulate our states of
alertness.*

explain the basics, we could use the Just Right Song as a "theme song" to help busy teachers, parents, and therapists introduce the Alert Program to students in classrooms and homes.

ABOUT THE TEST DRIVE SONGS:

Later that day, we took more time to consider how we could create a book that introduces the core concepts of the Alert Program through song. We realized that we wanted several songs that could help those with "too much to do, in too little time" teach self-regulation to their children:

✦ The Just Right Song is the main song that teaches students the engine analogy and sample ways to change how alert they feel.

✦ The Best Work song, with its bluesy swing, peaks students' interest in learning how easy it is to focus and pay attention when engines are in a just right level of alertness.

✦ The song Five Ways expands students' awareness of how to change their engine levels and how to choose from a larger variety of engine strategies.

✦ The Engine Song reinforces not only the engine vocabulary and strategies but adds a self-monitoring, social-emotional dimension. With phrases such as, *"make a good decision, yes I can!"* the song reminds children they can make good engine choices.

♪ The **Alive, Awake, Alert** song offers an ideal movement break for children's engines at school, at home, or in therapy settings.

♪ And the **Transition Songs** are instrumental recordings of selected *Test Drive* songs that can be used to support engines in times of transition. We've included four tracks that vary in duration: 30 seconds, one minute, two minutes, and three minutes. They are intended to be played as students change activities or focus, perhaps as they finish silent reading and prepare for their math lesson.

The songs on the CD are simple to use and require no special therapy equipment. Also, as you'll hear, there are no professional singers on any of these songs. You'll hear lots of enthusiastic kids' voices. And as lead vocals, you'll hear Sherry's and my "average, everyday" voices, along with an author of one of the songs, George Bendarczyk, PhD, CPsych. Our decision not to use professional singers'-songwriters' voices was very intentional; we want to encourage listeners to sing along whether or not they feel they have perfect pitch or sing off-key. We find that most children are not self-conscious in using their singing abilities, but many adults are. If you are a hesitant singer, turn up the volume on the CD and belt it out; you will thereby encourage your students to do the same. They will have fun singing along, perhaps without even realizing they are learning how to help their engines!

While singing the songs, students will be introduced to the very basics of self-regulation as their teachers, parents, and therapists "test-drive" the Alert Program. This book describes the essence of the Alert Program. After a trial run in introducing the Alert Program through music, we hope you will want to learn more about how to guide children's understanding of their self-regulation (see Appendix).

HOW TO USE THIS BOOK AND CD:

If you are new to the Alert Program, and you have time, we recommend reading all of the Alert Program products. If you are short on time, we strongly suggest you at least read this book in its entirety, prior to presenting the material to your students. With the numerous suggestions provided, you easily will be able to determine a teaching approach that will be successful with your students. The Alert Program Nuts and Bolts (Part II) and each of the Song Explanation sections (Part III), are important to read as you familiarize yourself with all the songs on the CD. Then you'll be ready to begin by first teaching the Just Right Song to your students. You will reap the benefits of the time spent preparing and reading the book, as you watch the children effortlessly embrace the engine analogy and self-regulation concepts.

If you are familiar with the Alert Program and you already have read the *Leader's Guide* and *Take Five*, you'll be in the unique position to take the information presented here "a step further" based on your previous experience in teaching your students about self-regulation. You probably will recognize the information contained in the Alert Program Nuts and Bolts section as a basic review. Be sure to at least browse through all the book's Side Notes to gain new Alert Program "tidbits." We suggest that you listen to all of the songs on the CD. Next choose which song you want to teach first to your students and read the section of the book that explains how to teach that song, including variations and suggestions. After you've tried one song, depending on your students' response and level of understanding, continue to select other songs and variations as suggested in the Song Explanations And Suggestions section.

Whether or not you (or your students) are familiar with the Alert Program, watch how quickly your students learn how to change their engines. As the song's lyrics describe, they may even start humming along, *"I do my best work, it's a great place to be. When my engine's just right, there's nothing stopping me!"*

TEST DRIVE: Introducing the Alert Program® Through Song

Alert Program
Nuts and Bolts

Part 2 two

Alert Program
Nuts and Bolts

As we mentioned in the Introduction, you can read more about the Alert Program® in our other publications. The purpose of this *Test Drive* book is to cover just the "nuts and bolts," in case you don't have time to read the *Leader's Guide, Take Five,* or *Introductory Booklet.* Obviously, the more familiar you are with self-regulation and the Alert Program the better, but to get you started, here are the basics:

WHAT THEORY SUPPORTS THE ALERT PROGRAM?

The Alert Program is based on the principles of sensory integration theory. A. Jean Ayres, PhD, OTR, FAOTA, spent over 30 years combining her knowledge of neuroscience and occupational therapy to create the theory, assessment, and treatment principles of sensory integration.

> "Sensory integration is the organization of sensation for use….The brain must organize all of these sensations if a person is to move and learn and behave normally. The brain locates, sorts, and orders sensations-somewhat as a traffic policeman directs moving cars. When sensations flow in a well-organized or integrated manner, the brain can use those sensations to form perceptions, behaviors, and learning. When the flow of sensations is disorganized, life can be like a rush-hour traffic jam." (Ayres, 1979, p. 5)

SIDE NOTE:

"Play is the work of children. Through play, children learn about themselves and the world around them. When all that they see, hear, and feel makes sense to them, a process of sensory integration occurs" (SII, 1991).

The Alert Program helps children who are typically developing as well as children who experience life "like a rush-hour traffic jam." These children have difficulty taking in and making sense of sensory information. "All day, every day, we receive information from our senses - touch, hearing, sight, taste, smell, body position, and movement and balance. Our brains must organize this information so that we can successfully function in all aspects of daily life - at home, at school, at play, at work, and during social interactions" (Koomar, 2003).

WHAT IS SELF-REGULATION?

Self-regulation is the ability to attain, maintain, or change how alert we feel, which influences our ability to engage in tasks or situations we encounter each day. When difficulties in self-regulation occur, we will have trouble changing the level of alertness we feel, which in turn will compromise optimal functioning.

WHY IS SELF-REGULATION IMPORTANT?

Self-regulation is the foundation of every goal a teacher, parent or therapist has for a child because, if one is not in an optimal state for learning, all learning can be more challenging. Self-regulation is important because it affects how well we function or perform the tasks and skills needed throughout our day. All of us (children and adults, typically and not so typically developing) can benefit from understanding about self-regulation and how our changing levels of alertness affect us throughout the day. When we are in an optimal state of alertness, we are more likely to experience success, which can lead to a sense of well-being, improve self-confidence, and enhance self-esteem.

SIDE NOTE:

As Dr. A. Jean Ayres' theory has grown and evolved, additional terminology has come into use (Miller, Cermak, Lane, Anzalone, Koomar, 2005). For example, Sensory Processing Disorder (SPD) is a diagnostic label being used to describe a "complex disorder of the brain that affects developing children and adults…in the way their brains interpret the information they take in and also how they act on that information with emotional, attentional, motor, and other responses" (Miller, 2006).

HOW DOES SELF-REGULATION
AFFECT LEARNING?

As adults, we spend a dreadful amount of time trying to teach when children's nervous systems are not in their optimal state for learning. If a teacher wants a child to learn a new math skill, the child's nervous system ideally should be in an optimal state to learn that skill. If it is not, the child will have more difficulty learning and demonstrating what has been learned. Furthermore, by overlooking the importance of self-regulation and its effect on learning, we may find ourselves dealing with behavioral outbursts that could have been avoided. When self-regulation is supported, children who struggle to pay attention are more "tuned in." By using engine strategies, teachers can help students regulate their nervous systems, setting them up for success. Repeatedly, we hear teachers, parents, and therapists say that the few minutes it takes to set up a nervous system for success is well worth the effort and ultimately saves time in not having to manage so many behavior problems.

HOW DO I TEACH SELF-REGULATION?

When first explaining the Alert Program to children, we (the authors), begin by saying, "If your body is like a car engine, sometimes it runs on high, sometimes it runs on low, and sometimes it runs just right." We usually go on to demonstrate what an engine in low might look like. We look lethargic, let our bodies droop toward the ground, and make little eye contact. We ask the children to show us what it feels like when their engines are in low gear. They will usually imitate us quite effortlessly.

TEST DRIVE: Introducing the Alert Program® Through Song

We go on to demonstrate an engine in high by showing with our bodies how it feels when we are hyperactive, wiggling our arms and legs, looking around the room, and breathing more quickly. We ask the children to show us their bodies in high gear. When you try this with children, don't be surprised if they get loud and a bit on the wild side as they show you their engines in high gear. Next we demonstrate what engines in a just right state might look like with our posture more upright and alert, breathing more regularly in a relaxed way, and smiling. We suggest you do a similar demonstration the first time you introduce the engine analogy to your students.

WHY THE ENGINE ANALOGY?

We came up with the engine analogy because it seems to be a straightforward way to talk about states of alertness. Remember, however, that we can use any descriptors that have <u>meaning to the child</u> and that conveys his or her inner experience of self-regulation.

The engine analogy is just one way but by no means the only way. For example, many children relate to the Winnie the Pooh story with the characters of Tigger typically in high gear, Eeyore in low gear, and Pooh in a just right gear.

We encourage those working with children to experiment to find what words work best to describe states of alertness such as:

⊹ colors (red for high, yellow for low, and green or blue for just right),

⊹ sounds (wooo for high, ugggh for low, and humming for just right),

♪ animals (cheetah for high, turtle for low, and bear for just right),

♪ transportation vehicles (jet plane for high, submarine for low, and "VW bug" car for just right), or

♪ dinosaurs (raptor for high, brontosaurus for low, and stegosaurus for just right).

Students can choose their own words which can be quite empowering. Two occupational therapists, in Pittsburgh, describe a shared language their middle schoolers developed to describe their states of alertness. Imagine how much these students felt a part of the group, fostering a sense of belonging, whenever they used their special words: "stoked" for high, "shot" for low, and "cruisin" for just right (Salls & Bucey, 2003).

WHAT ARE SELF-REGULATION STRATEGIES?

Using the engine analogy (or alternative terminology), students learn five ways to change engine levels: put something in your mouth, move, touch, look, and listen. We all self-regulate whether we are aware of the engine strategies we are employing or not. Remember "back in the day," when phones had cords and were often attached to walls? What did we do when the conversations lasted more than a few minutes? We would put a pencil to our mouth to chew (mouth category), pace a few feet back and forth as allowed by the cord (move category), twirl the cord with our fingers (touch category), or doodle on the phone book or nearby piece of paper (look category). We would do all of these things to try to give our bodies the sensorimotor input they need to concentrate in the phone conversation (listen category).

SIDE NOTE:

In their book, Fidget to Focus (2005), Roland Rotz, PhD, and Sarah E. Wright, MS, ACT, remind us, "Using sensory stimulation [engine strategies] to improve functioning dates back to our earliest civilizations. Whether the goal is to enhance pleasure, increase focus, improve health, or decrease pain, the intent of the sensory activity is to manipulate the body's cognitive, emotional, and behavioral systems in pursuit of that greater state of being. One of the earliest methods on influencing the body and mind through sensory experience was music…" (pp. 32-33).

TEST DRIVE: Introducing the Alert Program® Through Song

WHO CAN LEARN FROM THE ALERT PROGRAM?

Children who are typically and not so typically developing benefit from having the adults in their lives understand the importance of self-regulation. The Alert Program has been implemented by teachers in general education and special education classrooms, by parents in their homes, and by therapists in their therapy settings (as a "pull-out" therapy sessions) or co-leading Alert Program groups with teachers in classrooms ("inclusion" programs). The Alert Program can be successful with small or large groups of children and with individual students.

Non-independent self-regulators:

It is important to note that some young children will need help to self-regulate and some with special needs may never become independent in self-regulation. For example, if the family is driving six hours to go on vacation, a preschooler will need the adult to remember: "Oh, we're going on a long car ride. I better go fill up her backpack with some strategies to help her engine in the car." The parent may fill the backpack with a squishy fidget ball, an Etch-O-Sketch®, crunchy pretzels, and a cold cranberry juice slushy in a sippy cup. The parent may have found these were the best engine strategies for her daughter by experimenting with activities in *Take Five*.

More independent self-regulators:

Somewhat more independent children may need less adult assistance but still are not fully self-regulated. They may need adults to provide choices of strategies for them.

The adults consider what might be best for the children's engines and guide them to make good choices. For these types of children, we offer two choices, both of which will support their self-regulation and help them get to the just right level for the activity (e.g., "Do you want to crunch on some pretzels or carrots that I brought along for our car ride?")

Independent self-regulators:

In preparation for the car ride, a parent might say to a child who is independent in self-regulation, "We are going to go on a long car ride. It's often hard for you to sit that long in the car. Why don't you go to your room and fill your backpack with things that will help your engine in the car." A child who is independent in self-regulation will be able to go to his room, choose appropriate items like a Koosh® ball, headphones and music, an exercise water bottle, and his favorite kind of gum. Children learn to make these kinds of choices by completing the three stages and 12 steps of the Alert Program, outlined in the *Leader's Guide*.

WHO CAN BE AN ALERT PROGRAM LEADER?

Anyone can be a leader of the Alert Program. A teacher might be the Alert Program leader in the classroom. A parent, who is teaching the Alert Program to a child at home, might volunteer as a leader to assist the teacher in using the concepts in the classroom. A therapist (occupational therapist, social worker, psychologist, physical therapist, or speech and language pathologist), working with a student in their therapy setting to find out which strategies work best, might join with a teacher to co-lead an Alert Program group in the classroom. The Alert

Program is best implemented when all team members are familiar with the Alert Program concepts, the engine analogy, and engine strategy options.

Although anyone can be a leader of the program, we highly recommend that at least one person on the team has training in and is comfortable observing sensory processing difficulties. There are times when an engine could look like it is in low gear, but in fact, the child's nervous system is in danger of going into an autonomic reaction of "fight, flight, or fright." For this reason, it is critical that someone on the team be consulted to help with observations and problem solving to support self-regulation. (See Children With Special Needs: Handle With Care section).

We use the term "leader" to designate who is facilitating the self-regulation learning process, however, it might be more accurate to use the term "guide" or "collaborator" because it is a collaborative process. As children learn about their engines and begin discussing what they can do to change how alert they feel, they often "lead" or "guide" us to understand them better, if we are keen observers. And it is not uncommon to hear children reminding each other or gently suggesting, "Hey, you might want to do something for your engine. Looks like it's running on high gear right now. Maybe you could try a fidget toy or take a stretch break."

WHAT DO <u>YOU</u> DO TO SELF-REGULATE?

The Sensory-Motor Preference Checklist (Williams & Shellenberger, 1996, pp. 1-14) was designed for adults to become more aware of what they are doing to self-regulate. Our years of experience in using the Alert Program and teaching self-regulation have shown that the more all of us understand what strategies we use to change how alert we feel, the easier it is to observe and support children's self-regulation.

If you haven't filled out the checklist (on the following pages), please take a moment to do so. Consider what you do to help change how alert you feel throughout your day. What do you do in your morning routine to achieve the "just right" level of alertness so you can function well in your day? Do you need to brush your teeth first thing upon waking or grab a cup of coffee (mouth category)? Do you like to get up early and exercise right away to wake up (move category)? Or perhaps your body craves a steaming hot, pounding shower (touch category). Do you find it harder to wake up on a cloudy, rainy day and wish you could open the shades to let the sunshine awaken you (look category)? And do you like to wake up by turning on the TV or music, or do you prefer total silence in the morning (listen category)?

After you complete the Sensory-Motor Preference Checklist you will better understand your own engine needs and what supports your ability to self-regulate. We have found it extremely helpful to share with children (and those working and living with them) that "we all have engines." Some of our engines go higher and some go lower than others. Some are more challenging to understand or to find effective engine strategies. But we all benefit when we develop the vocabulary, such as the engine analogy, to better communicate our self-regulation needs. We hope that *Test Drive* will show you and your students how to explore and learn more about the Alert Program.

Sensory-Motor Preference
Checklist (for Adults)

DIRECTIONS: This checklist was developed to help adults recognize what strategies their own nervous systems employ to attain an appropriate state of alertness. Mark the items below that you use to increase (↑) or to decrease (↓) your state of alertness. You might mark both (↑↓) on some items. Others you might not use at all.

PUT SOMETHING IN YOUR MOUTH (ORAL MOTOR INPUT):

_ drink a milkshake
_ suck on hard candy
_ crunch or suck on ice pieces
_ tongue in cheek movements
_ "chew" on pencil / pen
_ chew on coffee swizzle sticks
_ take slow deep breaths
_ suck, lick, bite on your lips or the inside
  of your cheeks
_ drink carbonated drink
_ eat a cold popsicle
_ eat a pickle

_ chew gum
_ crunch on nuts / pretzels / chips
_ bite on nails / cuticle
_ eat popcorn / cut-up vegetables
_ eat chips and a spicy dip
_ smoke cigarettes
_ chew on buttons, sweatshirt strings or collars
_ whistle while you work
_ drink coffee / tea (caffeinated)
_ drink hot cocoa or warm milk
_ other:

MOVE (VESTIBULAR / PROPRIOCEPTIVE INPUT):

_ "doodle" while listening
_ rock in a rocking chair
_ shift or "squirm" in a chair
_ push chair back on 2 legs
_ aerobic exercise
_ isometrics / lift weights
_ rock own body slightly
_ scrub kitchen floor
_ roll neck and head slowly

_ sit with crossed legs and bounce one slightly
_ run / jog
_ ride bike
_ tap toe, heel or foot
_ dance
_ tap pencil / pen
_ yard work
_ stretch / shake body parts
_ other:

TOUCH (TACTILE INPUT):

_ twist own hair
_ move keys or coins in pocket with your hand
_ cool shower
_ warm bath
_ receive a massage
_ pet a dog or cat
_ drum fingers or pencil on table
_ rub gently on skin / clothes

Fidget with the following:
_ straw
_ paper clips
_ cuticle / nails
_ pencil / pen
_ earring or necklace
_ phone cord while talking
_ put fingers near mouth, eye, or nose
_ other:

LOOK (VISUAL INPUT)

_ open window shades after a boring movie in a
  classroom
_ watch a fireplace
_ watch fish tank
_ watch sunset / sunrise
_ watch "oil and water" toys

How do you react to:
_ dim lighting
_ fluorescent lighting
_ sunlight through bedroom window when
  sleeping
_ rose colored room
_ a "cluttered desk" when needing to concentrate

LISTEN (AUDITORY INPUT):

_ listen to Classical Music
_ listen to Hard Rock
_ listen to others "hum"
_ work in "quiet" room
_ work in "noisy" room
_ sing or talk to self

How do you react to:
_ scratch on a chalkboard
_ "squeak" of a mechanical pencil
_ fire siren
_ waking to an unusual noise
_ dog barking (almost constantly)

QUESTIONS TO PONDER

1. Review this Sensory-Motor Preference Checklist. Think about what you do in a small subtle manner to maintain an appropriate alert level that a child with a less mature nervous system may need to do in a larger more intense way.

2. Notice which types of sensory input are comforting to your nervous system and which types of sensory input bother your nervous system. Are your items clustered in a certain category of sensory input?

3. Consider how often (frequency), how long (duration), how much (intensity), and with what rhythm (fast, slow, uneven or even) you use these inputs to change your state of alertness.

4. When you are needing to concentrate at your work space, what sensory input do you prefer to work most efficiently?

   a) What do you put in or around your mouth? (Example: food, drink, gum, etc.)

   b) What do you prefer to touch? (Example: clothing, texture of chair, fidgeting with objects, etc.)

   c) What types of movement do you use? (Example: rock in chair or movement breaks to stretch or walk, etc.)

   d) What are your visual preferences? (Example: natural lighting from window, use of a lamp, brightly colored walls. Are you an "in" person working best with your desk cleared off or an "out" person whose desk is piled high with papers, etc.)

   e) What auditory input do you use? (Example: do you listen to music while you work? If so, what type of beat? Do you like to talk to yourself or others and work at the same time? Do you prefer a quiet environment?, etc.)

SIDE NOTE:

As discussed in greater detail in the Leader's Guide, the Alert Program is taught in three stages with 12 Mile Markers, along with the five ways to change engine levels. If you are not familiar with the Leader's Guide here is a summary:

STAGE ONE: Identifying Engine Speeds

1. *Students learn labels for the engine levels (high, low, and just right).*

2. *Adults describe their own engine levels to students.*

3. *Students develop awareness of the feel of their own engine speeds, with the help of adults' guidance.*

4. *Students learn to identify and label levels for themselves.*

5. *Students label levels for themselves, outside the Alert Program sessions.*

STAGE TWO: Experimenting with Methods to Change Engine Speeds

6. *Leaders introduce sensorimotor methods to change engine levels.*

7. *Leaders identify students' sensorimotor preferences and sensory hypersensitivities.*

8. *Students begin experimentation with choosing effective strategies.*

STAGE THREE: Regulating Engine Speeds

9. *Students choose strategies independently.*

10. *Students use strategies independently, outside Alert Program sessions.*

11. *Students learn to change engine levels when options are limited.*

12. *Students continue receiving support.*

TEST DRIVE: Introducing the Alert Program® Through Song

Songs Explanations and Suggestions

Part 3 three

Test Drive
Songs

TEST DRIVE: Introducing the Alert Program® Through Song

Just Right
Song

JUST RIGHT SONG

Sometimes my engine runs high… woooo
Sometimes my engine runs… looooow
Sometimes my engine runs… Just Right!

There are things I can do to change my engine
Put something in my mouth…
Take a big, deep breath… aaaaaahhhhhhhh,
That can help my engine feel… Just Right!

There are things I can do to change my engine
Move and push and pull… ugggggg.
March and twiiiiiiiiiiirl and jump, jump, jump, jump.
That can help my engine feel… Just Right!

Sometimes my engine runs high… woooo
Sometimes my engine runs… looooow
Sometimes my engine runs… Just Right!

There are things I can use to change my engine
A fidget in my hand…
Brighten up my room…
Listen to some tunes… hum, hum, hum.
That can help my engine feel… Just Right!

Sometimes my engine runs high… woooo
Sometimes my engine runs… looooow
Sometimes my engine runs… Just Right!

What can I do to change my engine?
Put something in my mouth…
Take a big, deep breath… aaaaaahhhhhhhh

Move and push and pull… ugggggg.
March and twiiiiiiiiiiirl and jump, jump, jump, jump,
A fidget in my hand…
Brighten up my room…
Listen to some tunes… hum, hum, hum…
That can make my engine feel…
Just right, Just Right, Just right, Juuuuuuuuuust Right!!!!

TEST DRIVE: Introducing the Alert Program® Through Song

Just Right
Song Explanation

Track 1: Test Drive Introduction
Track 2: Chorus Only (slow tempo to learn motions)
Track 3: Novice Version (slow tempo with verses)
Track 4: Emerging Version (chorus, verses, and summary)
Track 5: Expert Version (chorus, verses, summary and extra
            challenging phrases)

BACKGROUND:

The *Just Right Song's* original lyrics and melody were written by Elise Dirske, OTR/L, who has helped campers at Camp Avanti in Hudson, Wisconsin for many years. Camp Avanti is a unique, one-week camp for children with sensory processing challenges. Yearly, volunteer therapists, like Elise, gather from across the States and from other countries to create a successful camp experience through the use of typical camp activities, supported by therapeutic interventions. Elise wrote this song to help her campers understand their engines and the strategies to use while engaged in crafts, canoeing, swimming, archery, etc. She found the song was a simple way to help children learn about what they could do to change their engines so they could get the most out of camp. Elise shares, "The kids really responded well to the music, rhythm, and lyrics. It captured their attention and taught them the Alert Program® concepts in a fun, alternative way."

When we received Elise's song for review, we added a bit here and there, after singing the song with many different age groups. We watched the students experiment with a variety of motions and observed what helped them best to learn. We were thrilled to see how rapidly students could learn about their engines through the words and motions of this one song.

TRACKS OF THE JUST RIGHT SONG:

We feel that this Just Right Song has so much potential to teach the essence of the Alert Program that we decided to provide you with multiple versions. If this is the only song that you use on the CD, we're confident your students will soon be singing along and engaging in engine strategies that will support their ability to focus and attend.

The Just Right Song was recorded in successive degrees of difficulty so that a teacher (or parent or therapist) needs no musical abilities; the tracks used in succession will teach the song step by step:

✦ On the first track, Mary Sue and Sherry introduce the *Test Drive* CD.

✦ The second track is the "Chorus Only Version." It is a recording of the chorus without the verses. This song correlates to Stage One in the *Leader's Guide* when students first learn about engines running on high, low, and just right (before learning about engine strategies in Stage Two).

Many educators are using curriculums which categorize children's skill development as Novice, Emerging, and Expert. In keeping with that theme, we developed tracks for the Just Right Song *that reflect these three skill levels. In addition, a Chorus Only Version is included for those students who may not become independent in self-regulation or who may not be developmentally old enough to choose their own engine strategies.*

♦ The third track is the "Novice Version" with chorus and verses. This version (like the Chorus Only Version) has a slow tempo and few instruments to keep it simple for young children and those with special needs (especially those who have difficulty making sense of complicated auditory information).

♦ The fourth track is the "Emerging Version" with a faster tempo than the Novice Version but with less complicated instruments, lyrics, and motions than the "Expert Version."

♦ The fifth track is the Expert Version, intended for older students who want an extra challenge to remember all of the ways to change engines levels while doing the motions. This summary is sung in a lively rendition, including motions and extra phrases to spark the enthusiastic listener's ear to follow along.

LEARNING ABOUT ENGINE LEVELS IN THE CHORUS:

As mentioned previously, students learn to recognize engine levels as they do the motions in the Track 2, Chorus Only Version (see "Just Right Song Motions" chart). Even if children are unfamiliar with the engine analogy, they quickly grasp the concepts and will enjoy acting out what engines in high, low, and just right look like. Here is a more detailed explanation of the chorus lyrics:

"Sometimes my engine runs high."
Do you know these children? The ones whose engines tend to run on high? They seem to move more than other children and they may feel wild or out of control. Not many

adults (or kids) have trouble identifying engines in high gear. These children often end up in the principal's office or at least are "well known" throughout the school. They most likely are having difficulty concentrating on school work and sadly often do not feel good about themselves. The Alert Program vocabulary can help to de-stigmatize these children. For this to happen we must remind adults and children that we all have engines; some of us have engines that just run a little higher or lower than others. Edward Hallowell, MD, (2006) reminds children with Attention Deficit Disorders and other disabilities that they have "a gift, but a gift that is difficult to unwrap" (p. 104). As adults we are all challenged to find ways to help children feel positive about themselves and search for their strengths and gifts that may indeed be difficult to unwrap.

"Sometimes my engine runs low."
These are the children that often don't get noticed in classrooms at first glance because they tend to be quiet and usually their behaviors are less noticeable. They are not apt to be sent to the principal's office for boisterous behavioral outbursts like students whose engines frequently run in high gear. Instead, these students are socially more withdrawn and may look lethargic or droopy. However, when engines are in low gear, then irritability and resistance is common, so they can also appear non-compliant. When their engines are supported to be in a just right gear, they more easily follow directions and willingly participate in activities.

TEST DRIVE: Introducing the Alert Program® Through Song

"Sometimes my engine runs just right."
When in a just right gear, a child will be more focused, attentive, and alert. In a classroom, a teacher may observe that, when a student is in a just right level (an optimal state for learning), it is easiest to teach a new reading concept. A parent, who wants to help her daughter do her homework, for example, will find homework time will go more smoothly if the child is in an optimal state for studying. And likewise, a speech therapist working on articulation may find a child is more likely to be able to produce the "r" sound when in a just right state.

It's important to note that technically we cannot know for sure whether a child's nervous system is in high, low, or just right without physiological testing. All we can do is make our best guess based on observable posture and muscle tone (droopy or tense), activity level (hypo or hyperactive) and the quality of interactions (engaged or disengaged). Remember, the goal is not for children to become perfectly accurate in labeling engine levels but for them to learn how to change how alert they feel so they can function best.

LEARNING ENGINE STRATEGIES THROUGH THE VERSES:

As they sing the verses, children are encouraged to try some of the strategies they might use to make learning easier. There are endless options of strategies for changing alert levels, but the following are sample strategies that will be introduced in the Just Right Song:

Put something in my mouth.
Take a big deep breath.
Move and push and pull.
March and twirl and jump.
A fidget in my hand.
Brighten up my room.
Listen to some tunes.
That can help my engine feel… Just Right!

When children learn the Alert Program, as outlined in the *Leader's Guide*, they experiment with the five ways to change engine levels (mouth, move, touch, look, listen). In this song, we chose examples of engine strategies for the verses that require the least amount of equipment or materials. We took the "bare bones" approach, but there are numerous possibilities of sensorimotor strategies, some of which are described later in the Five Ways song.

Listed below are the engine strategies and motions used in the Just Right Song. The verses begin with: *"There are things I can do to change my engine…"*

TEST DRIVE: Introducing the Alert Program® Through Song

"Put something in my mouth."
As the children sing this line, they can chew, tug, and pull on straws here (see Optional Use of Straws paragraph later in this section) or, if straws are not available, they can make silly mouth sounds.

"Take a big, deep breath."
Encourage students to inhale deeply. Then, they exhale slowly while saying, "Aaaahhhh."

"Move and push and pull."
The children's arms reach out in a "pushing motion" and then arms curl into the chest in a "pulling motion." While doing these motions, they groan saying, "Uuuuugggggh."

An option for older students is to do isometrics, a form of muscle-building exercises that are usually performed without motion. Students can push palms together as they sing "push." And while they sing "pull," the students imitate the hand position of an opera singer. (Curl the fingers on each hand to form a semi-circle. Rotate one hand toward the body and one hand away from the body. Interlock fingers and pull apart.)

"March and twirl and jump."
While singing these words, younger children will probably only have the coordination and enough time to twirl in a circle and jump. Older children may be able to march in place, twirl, and jump. This line of the song includes jumping because it helps give input to the muscles and joints that can prevent escalation of engines into high gear. If a child has difficulty self-regulating after twirling (engine goes into high), you may want to encourage that

child to jump only and not twirl. And if a child happens to be listening to the Just Right Song while sitting in a chair or riding along in a car, he can still move his upper body in a circular motion and "jump" (or attempt to bounce) in his seat in time to the music.

"A fidget in my hand."
If using straws, use the kind with a flexible neck, so children can wiggle and twist them in this part of the song. If straws are not available, children move their fingers, pretending to play with a fidget toy.

"Brighten up my room."
Children slowly stretch arms to the ceiling, then bring their arms back to their sides, while looking up to the sky (or lights in the room). This line of the song can be a bit confusing to some children; as they learn more about the five ways to change engine levels, more discussion can follow. (See Five Ways Explanation and Suggestion section.)

"Listen to some tunes."
Children point to their ears and hum while singing this line of the song. Later in this section, suggestions will be made how to lead a discussion about music preferences and how they affect engine levels.

SIDE NOTE:

Christy Kennedy, OTR/L, in Atlanta, was one of the first to try out the Just Right Song. *She shares, "Having this* Just Right Song *seemed to make my words about engines (their speeds and behaviors related to them) more believable. The categories of 'engine helpers' were easy for the children to remember as presented in the song."*

Christy runs "Engine Camps" each summer for children aged four to nine years old with sensory processing challenges. After this year's day camp was over, she emailed, "I can't say enough wonderful things about the Just Right Song. *I sent home the words and parents are reporting that their children are singing and saying the lyrics on their own. In response to questions from their moms as to, 'What can you do to help your Engine?'… [Parents heard answers] such as, 'A fidget in my hand.'*

Even though Christy has implemented the Alert Program with numerous groups of children over the past decade, she commented about using the song, "I have NEVER seen the 'Engine Concept' carry over as fast with a group of children, many to whom the concept is new!" (personal communication, June 2006).

HOW TO TEACH THE JUST RIGHT SONG:

Here are some suggestions for teaching the Just Right Song and the basics of the Alert Program. We'll go into more detail with this song than with the others in this book, since this is our "theme song" and it can be used in many ways to support learning about engines. First, before you begin, we encourage you to familiarize yourself with all tracks of the Just Right Song, and read through the suggestions below.

TRACK 1 (Introduction):
♪ Listen to Track 1, where we explain the purpose of the CD.

TRACK 2 (Chorus Only):
♪ Begin by introducing the engine concept to your students by saying something like: "Today we're going to hear a new song. It's about what we can do to make learning easier. Let's listen to the song to learn how our body is like a car engine." Most likely you will want the children standing to sing the song so they will be able to move their bodies more freely than while seated.

♪ Be prepared for great enthusiasm as they act out what it might look like if their engines are in a high, low, or just right gear. Usually the most enthusiasm is seen in the children as they act out high gear, especially for the first time. Allow plenty of time for the students to enjoy showing you how well they already understand the concept! It will be time well spent so they can then better focus on learning the words of the song.

♦ You may want to play Track 2 several times for your students to practice learning the words to the chorus. Some children who are learning the Alert Program following the *Leader's Guide* may be at Stage One, where they are just learning about their engines and may not be ready to go on to Track 3. If you feel your students have grasped the concept of engine levels and are familiar with the words of the chorus, go on to Track 3.

TRACK 3 (Novice Version):

♦ Track 3 (Novice Version) includes the chorus and verses. Tell your students that in this longer version of the song they will learn the verses. Ask them to listen carefully to ways that they can learn to change their engine levels. Explain that there are motions for the words in the verses and the summary. Ask them to just listen the first time you play the song. Then the second time, demonstrate what motions they can do. (See "Just Right Song Motions" chart.)

TRACK 4 (Emerging Version):

♦ Explain to your students that this version of the song is a little faster and it might be a little trickier to do all of the motions. Play Track 4 several times until the students are familiar with the Emerging Version of the song and the motions.

♦ If you feel your students are familiar with the words and motions of the Emerging Version, you may decide to go on to Track 5, the Expert Version. On the other hand, you may find some young children or some with special needs enjoy singing this version (Track 4) more than singing Track 5.

⊕ Caution: We want to ensure success for children whose bodies are not ready yet to master the advanced words and motions in the Expert Version. Even typically developing third graders often find the Expert Version too challenging.

TRACK 5 (Expert Version):

⊕ You might introduce the Expert Version by saying: "You are doing such a great job learning this song. Now that you know the words and motions to the chorus and the verses, I think you're ready for a challenge. Boys and girls, listen carefully to the last part of the song. It will be fun to see if we can sing all of the words and do the motions, too. Ready?"

> NOTE: In our youth, we enjoyed the challenge of singing Rudolph the Red-Nosed Reindeer with extra phrases. Remember singing, *"Like a light bulb"* after the line: *"Rudolph the Red-Nosed Reindeer had a very shiny nose"*? We added this type of phrasing after each line of the verses in the Expert Version. As the children learn the summary, they may need extra practice time to fit all of the words and motions in at the faster tempo (but that's half the fun!).

⊕ Play Track 5 and sing along with as much animation in your voice and as much gesturing as possible. Pretend you are a chorus director, even if you are not very comfortable singing in front of a group. Go ahead, enjoy yourself, because the students surely will. The more you cue the students when they should do the motions or insert the extra phrases the more quickly they will learn the song and feel confident in singing along.

OPTIONAL USE OF STRAWS:

When we teach the Just Right Song to students we give them straws to use when they sing *"Put something in my mouth"* and *"A fidget in my hand."* We have found that when students use the straw in the song, they learn how such strategies can affect their engines. Whenever we first introduce a strategy to students, even something as simple as a straw, we always take a few minutes to discuss with the students and adults, how and why we will be using it.

For example, we were fortunate to have the opportunity to "kid test" the Just Right Song at a school-wide assembly. When we introduced the idea of using a straw to the whole elementary school, we sent out a memo to ensure that the teachers understood the Alert Program basics (see Appendix).

We wrote the memo because after our years of using the Alert Program, we find that communication is essential. If we don't take the time to help adults understand the basic Alert Program theory, then we may not be able to fully support the child's use of the strategy or engine vocabulary. Surely, we don't want a child to learn about her engine at school and then go home to an unsuspecting parent, announcing, "Hey, I learned how to get <u>high</u> at school today!" We also don't want to set up a child for failure when he learns about the Alert Program at home, then "gets in trouble" for using a strategy at school because the teacher is unfamiliar with the engine concepts. On the other hand, if the teacher is informed that a child is experimenting with engine strategies at home (discovering, for example, that chewing on a straw makes

SIDE NOTE:

Depending on the age and needs of your students, you'll determine which Just Right Song track is best. The text in this section was written for those who will be teaching all verses of the song, and there are numerous other ways to introduce this song using the different tracks. For example, with typical fourth grade students, you may choose to skip the Chorus Only and Novice Version, simply play the Emerging Version once, and then immediately move onto the Expert Version. If you are teaching those with special needs, you may play the Chorus Only Version repeatedly and then introduce the Novice Version and never play the Emerging or Expert Versions.

studying for a spelling test easier), she can support him to do his best on the spelling test. The *Introductory Booklet,* written for the purpose of explaining the Alert Program's key concepts, is one of many useful tools for fostering good communication and self-regulation understanding among team members.

AN EXAMPLE OF SELF-REGLUATION AT A SCHOOL ASSEMBLY:

The school where we "kid-tested" the Just Right Song typically holds their assemblies in the mornings. On the day we were teaching the Just Right Song, the assembly just happened to be at the end of the day, due to standardized testing. Think about your students (and other teachers) after a long day of standardized testing, and you'll easily imagine what we saw: Students were sitting on the gymnasium floor, shifting their weight left and right, putting fingers to their mouth, playing with their hair and jewelry, rubbing hands on their clothes, touching their neighbor's clothes, moving their feet, and at least one child was sucking her thumb. The teachers were shocked that the students couldn't sit still and pay attention. Many commented to us that "usually the students are so attentive!"

Being observers of self-regulation, we were not surprised to see that most students' engines were dipping into low gear after a long day of challenging seatwork. We expected they would need to move more and use more strategies to self-regulate. It seemed like the perfect time to "kid-test" our song and give those poor bodies some options to get back to a just right level. The song and its strategies were well-received and most students (and teachers) seemed to have an easier time focusing on the remaining 15 minutes of the assembly. But let's remember that when children or adults are tired, ill, or have other medical conditions, engine strategies may not be enough. Some of those kindergartners probably just needed a nap when they got home from school that day!

DISCUSSION AFTER SINGING THE JUST RIGHT SONG:

After teaching the Just Right Song, you might encourage an in-depth discussion about engines, such as," I remember one time when I was running late and rushing to a doctor's appointment. My engine felt like this." (Show hyperactivity with your face and body.) "Who can tell me about a time when your engine was running on high?"

To facilitate a discussion about a low state of alertness you might say, "For me, when my engine is in low gear, I feel like my mind and body are trying to move through molasses." (Demonstrate a hypo-activity level, using facial expression and droopy body posture.) "When do you remember feeling like your engine was in low?"

In describing a just right level of alertness you could say something like, "After singing this song, my engine feels just right." (Show students with your expression of face and body.) "Do you remember a time at home or at school when you felt like your engine was running just right? Was it easy or hard to focus and concentrate?"

SIDE NOTE:

Marci Laurel, MA, CCC-SLP, works in the Autism Resource Team in the Albuquerque Public Schools. She reminds us that the children who "can easily use words for verbal expression, problem-solving, and understanding ideas learn differently than those whose auditory and verbal systems are not strong channels for learning" (personal communication, July 2006). Many of the examples in this book will be for those children who can verbally express and understand language easily. Throughout the book, you'll read sample conversations a teacher might initiate with her students (or parents with their sons or daughters) who are not struggling with these language skills. We will also intersperse a few examples [see "Simplified Language Examples" in text] that do not rely as heavily on language to highlight how you might explain these concepts to younger children or those who find speaking and/or listening more challenging. (Consult with a speech and language pathologist for more suggestions.)

Help the students share their experiences in this type of discussion. And more importantly, throughout the day, notice and make comments about how your engine is feeling. If you feel your engine is going into high gear, explain this to your students. You might be surprised at how willing they will be to help you out when they hear you say, "My engine is going into high gear right now. My ears are getting bothered by the loud sounds. It's not wrong for you to be talking to your neighbor while you are making your Valentines, but right now, if you could help my engine, I'd appreciate a little more quiet. And I'm going to do some chair push-ups to get the heavy work that my engine needs. Anybody else want to join me in doing some chair push-ups for your engine?" In addition to the students learning from the adult's modeling about self-regulation strategies, they learn about cooperating and supporting one another.

[Simplified Language Example: With a child who has difficulty understanding and responding to language, the teacher might say, "Ooooh, my ears hurt. Quiet, please. Do push-ups?"]

In discussions, it's best to not begin by asking questions such as, "How's your engine running right now?" but to first make a statement about your own engine level. Just as children learn about feelings by adult modeling, adults facilitate better understanding of self-regulation when they talk first about their own state of alertness without asking questions. (The *Leader's Guide* contains more information about when and how to begin asking students questions about their engines.)

Along with adult modeling, you can make comments that teach the child about his or her engine by making a statement (still not a question), such as, "Looks like your engine is on high right now. I can tell because it seems like your body is moving more and it seems like it is hard to get your work done."

Please be very careful so as not to use body language or a harsh voice that might imply that the student is wrong. We find students learn about their engines best when adults use a neutral tone of voice, reflecting curiosity, rather than shame or blame. This is a concept that most of us would agree with in theory, but let's be honest: when our own engines are on high, it can be a challenge to remember that we must be patient when teaching children about their engines.

One last caution here: Rarely, do we find agreement among a group of people about our choices for sensorimotor strategies. Because many of us are unaware of how we self-regulate, we can have difficulty negotiating with our students, or even our friends and loved ones, about engine strategies.

For example, you might ask your students: "What kind of music do you like to play for your engines to run just right?" Some adults and children like loud, bouncy music. Others like soft, smooth music. You might think of an example to share with your students about a time when you needed to compromise about your sensorimotor preferences, such as, "I really like classical music. It keeps my engine running just right for work. Once, when I was sharing an office with a co-worker, I had to learn to cooperate. We each liked different radio stations. Her engine seemed to go into low pretty easily, so she liked rock and roll music. My engine went up into high when I listened to rock and roll. What do you think we did?" This is a fine opportunity to discuss celebrating our diversities and learning how to communicate and cooperate with others.

JUST RIGHT
SONG MOTIONS

LYRICS:	MOTIONS:	NOVICE/ EMERGING SAY:	EXPERT ONLY SAY:
Sometimes my engine runs high	Shake hands above head wildly	Woooo	Woooo
Sometimes my engine runs low	After words, droop down looking lethargic	Looooow	Looooow
Sometimes my engine runs just right	Standing upright and looking perky	Smiling	Snap fingers (or thumbs up sign)
Put something in my mouth	Tug on straw in mouth	Quiet here because mouth is busy	"Helps me concentrate"
Take a big, deep breath	Deeply inhale and exhale slowly	Aaaahhhh	Aaaahhhh
That can make my engine feel just right	Standing upright and looking perky	Smiling	Snap fingers (or thumbs up sign)
Move and push and pull	Palms together to push, then saying "pull," grasp fingers to pull apart like singing opera (isometrics)	Uggggggg	Uggggggg… "Heavy Work!"
March and twirl and jump	Stomp feet, twirl around then jump several times	Jump, jump, jump, jump	"Jump with the beat, jump!"
A fidget in my hand	Bend straw in hands	Quietly move hands	"I like the squishy one"
Brighten up my room	Slowly stretch arms to the ceiling then back to sides	Quietly move arms	"Got my shades on" while putting fingers to eyes like glasses
Listen to some tunes	Point to ears and hum	Hum, hum, hum	"Bring on the tunes!"

TEST DRIVE: Introducing the Alert Program® Through Song

Best Work
Song

BEST WORK

I do my best work and it's a great place to be,
When my engine's Just Right, there's nothin' stopping me.
So easy to find, more ways to show
All those around me, just what I know.
Now, does my body, spend all day here?
Nuh-uh. We all do things, to change our gear.

Amazing how low, my engine can go
When I'm feelin' brain dead, there's no one running the show.
My energy's going, down the drain
Simple school work, man, it feels like a pain.
A jump start's needed, to get me in gear
Or else doin' this work, could take all year!

I do my best work and it's a great place to be,
When my engine's Just Right, there's nothin' stopping me.
So easy to find, more ways to show
All those around me, just what I know.
Now, does my body, spend all day here?
Nuh-uh. We all do things, to change our gear.

Downside of my engine, being on high
Well it's makin' it tough for me to just get by.
Plenty of speed, but it's the antsy kind
If I need to focus, I'm in a bind.

To change my engine (to change my engine),
I know what it takes (I know what it takes)
Won't catch me makin', (Won't catch me makin'),
Won't catch me makin', no engine mistakes.

'Cause, I do my best work and it's a great place to be,
When my engine's Just Right, there's nothin' stopping me.
So easy to find, more ways to show
All those around me, just what I know.
Now, does my body, spend all day here?
Nuh-uh. We all do things, to change our gear.

TEST DRIVE: Introducing the Alert Program® Through Song

Best Work
Song Explanation

SIDE NOTE:

I (Sherry) am fortunate to have worked with many bright, sincere, well-intentioned, and fun-loving children whose engines rarely ran optimally for learning in school. Sadly, many of these students had low self-esteem with somewhat negative "self-talk." I remember one fourth grade boy-we'll call him Kevin-who was new to the engine concepts. He was receiving OT services in a pull-out group session. I went to his regular education classroom to pick him up for our group. As he was closing the door to the classroom, he said to me, "You saved my life! I was just about to get in trouble in there!" It struck me that Kevin had no idea how he could avoid getting in trouble. In his mind, it was inevitable. He didn't know how to use engine strategies yet. I wrote the Best Work lyrics with Kevin (and others like him) in mind. I wanted to replace negative self-talk with positive lyrics such as, "To change my engine, I know what it takes." I wish back then I had Best Work and the other Test Drive songs for Kevin because with his enthusiasm for life, he surely would have embraced the line, "When my engine's just right, there's nothin' stoppin' me!"

CHORUS:

Sherry wrote this song to help students understand that we all (adults and children) have engines and we all fluctuate somewhere between high, low, and just right speeds throughout the day. As adults, we want to show children how to get their engines to the just right level, where it's easiest to demonstrate their knowledge. The Best Work song's chorus reminds children that when in a just right speed *"I do my best work"* and then it's *"so easy to find more ways to show, all those around me just what I know."* Although the Alert Program® aims to teach children how to get to the just right level for a particular task, Sherry also wanted children to understand that it's not practical, or necessary, to stay in an optimal state of alertness all day long. Therefore, the chorus emphasizes, *"Now, does my body spend all day here? Nuh-uh. We all do things to change our gear."*

VERSES:

The first verse of Best Work teaches the students that when engines are in low, it's much more difficult to focus and get schoolwork completed. One line of this song explains: *"doin' this work, could take all year!"* If we don't give our bodies a movement break or use another engine strategy, completing schoolwork or any other task will take longer as our focus wanes and our efficiency decreases. We emphasize to children and their adults that by taking a movement break, we can often gain time and attention. Using an engine strategy allows children to return to an optimal state for learning. And it can often avoid behavioral outbursts caused by bodies not getting the stimulation needed to focus and concentrate. Of course, self-regulation or poor sensory processing is not the only reason children have difficulty paying attention, but brain-behavior research tells us that offering movement breaks or other sensorimotor strategies often can be useful (Lane, 2002).

After sitting for extended periods of time, we all need to "take five." As mentioned in *Take Five*, we cannot "sit still and pay attention." We can sit still or pay attention. Try an experiment: while you are reading this paragraph, try to not move your legs or feet. Try to not play with your cuticle or rub your hands on your clothing. Do not put your fingers near your mouth or touch your jewelry or mustache. Don't play with your hair or buttons on your shirt. Don't wiggle your toes or move your tongue in your mouth. Don't do any of the things you typically do for self-regulation. You may not even be aware of the things you do until you are asked to stop. Are you able to concentrate without moving some part of your body? Now consider if you were not allowed to do these types of self-regulation strategies for a longer period of time. Would you have trouble continuing to read and focus? "Sitting still" makes the brain feel like it is in a type of sensorimotor deprivation, and typically we will have difficulty paying attention.

If as adults, we can't "sit still" to read a page of this book, imagine a child in a typical day at school. We know that there is a difference between a child's and an adult's nervous system: a child's nervous system needs more frequent breaks, longer breaks, or breaks with more intensity of movement than an adult's nervous system does. Unfortunately, some adults base their predictions of how long or how often a child needs an engine strategy on their own adult needs (assuming what they need to self-regulate as adults will be the same as what a child needs). In fact, think about a typical, traditional classroom. Who is standing up at the front of the room, getting the most amount of movement? Yes, the teacher's engine is often in a just right state while the children's engines are not. Yet, the students are expected to sit quietly in their seats while the teacher gets to move around the room. Informed teachers carefully observe their students' engine levels while they are teaching to see when the students need an engine strategy. Many teachers (and parents) find that by "taking five," children gain five, 10, 20, or even 30 minutes of concentration.

Marci Laurel, the speech and language pathologist mentioned earlier, shares her experience supporting a child who needs more input, more often than the average child to succeed in school:

> "When dealing with challenging children who need very frequent and intense sensory input, I work with teachers first to track how long the child can maintain attention (for example, in Circle Time) before seeking sensory input (such as jumping up

and down, touching other children, or making noises, any of which might be interpreted as 'behavior'). Once we figure out how long a child can focus and what type of sensory input they are seeking [mouth, move, touch, look, or listen category], we then work to provide the child with supportive sensory input at a given time interval, theoretically before the behavior starts."

Marci tells about a child we'll call Bobby. After tracking how long he could attend in Circle Time, the teacher determined that Bobby usually had an aggressive outburst after about 12 minutes among his peers. He appeared to be seeking movement for his engine, so the team decided to try offering heavy work activities more frequently throughout his day, such as bouncing on a Hippity Hop ball or pushing a weighted play grocery cart. Marci goes on to say,

> "Initially, Bobby did best when he had the opportunity to select from one of two heavy work activities every 10 minutes on a choice board [visual pictures that Bobby points to, indicating his choice]. The staff was initially concerned this would interrupt his learning. However, his teacher noticed that he was able to work in a more focused way during those 10 minutes, and the occurrence of aggressive behavior decreased substantially. Offering frequent engine strategies seemed to be the best way to allow Bobby to learn and to prevent outbursts of 'behavior.'

Bobby was less disruptive to classroom activities than when he didn't get the needed sensory input. Over time,

TEST DRIVE: Introducing the Alert Program® Through Song

the staff was able to help Bobby to work for longer periods of time without a break. They developed better ideas about which strategies worked best for his engine and they provided consistent positive behavioral supports" (personal communication, August 2006).

DISCUSSION AFTER SINGING THE BEST WORK SONG:

For some students, we have found it is helpful to <u>prove</u> that we do our best when our engines are in an optimal state of alertness. You might have a conversation with students about the line in **Best Work:** When my engine is in high gear, *"if I need to focus, I'm in a bind."* Ask them if, when their engines are in high gear, they can do their best at something they enjoy doing, such as shooting basketball hoops or winning at their favorite computer game. Help the students to identify what they enjoy doing, and select a task for which they can record their accuracy. Be sure to encourage students to choose an activity that has meaning to them, one at which they want to succeed.

For example, consider a student whose engine tends to pop up into high gear and who loves to shoot basketball hoops. You could encourage her to set up an experiment to see how many hoops she can make in an allotted amount of time, when her engine is in high vs. just right state. Make a simple form for recording the number of hoops when she's in high and when she's in just right (and perhaps when she's in low, if that's a common state she experiences in her day). Then help the student to get into an extremely high state for several minutes, perhaps by playing loud rock and roll music or running around

SIDE NOTE:

We had the good fortune to have some excellent musicians in our band "backing us up" as we sang this **Best Work** *song. Students can create their own "band" by using natural instruments such as a five gallon metal bucket, milk jug, aluminum soda pop cans filled with beans and duct-taped closed, wooden spoons, etc. Your students may want to write their own music score to create their own unique song.*

the room in circles while shouting. Or ask the student what makes her engine go into high and then have her engage in that activity for several minutes. Then, ask the student to shoot hoops. Record the results. Next, the student should do some kind of heavy work activity for several minutes: pushing on a wall, pulling a towel or rope, carrying a heavy box of books, or doing chair push-ups, perhaps while listening to classical music. When you are confident that the student's engine is back to an optimal level for basketball, ask her to shoot hoops again and record her results. You may want to repeat the experiment over several days to prove to the student that she will have more accuracy and focus if her engine is in an optimal state for the task. In singing this song and learning more about the Alert Program, the student will find out that when *"my engine's just right, there's nothin' stopping me… to change my engine, I know what it takes."*

SIDE NOTE:

One therapist shared with us how much her clients enjoy her asking the question, "What does your mom's or dad's engine look like when it goes into high?" Or, "What happens when their engine goes into low?" They often giggle and respond with surprising accuracy. One child also made the connection that his father watches TV at night to put himself to sleep. And we (the authors) frequently suggest that students interview their parent or teacher while taking notes on a Sensory-Motor Preference Checklist. In these ways, children understand that "we all have engines" and we all do things to change our engine speeds. These types of discussion lead to an appreciation and respect for our sensorimotor differences and preferences, thereby fostering respect and a deeper understanding of one another.

TEST DRIVE: Introducing the Alert Program® Through Song

Five Ways
Song

FIVE WAYS

Five ways, we've got five ways
To maximize your days.
Mouth, Move, Touch, Look, Listen
And find your way.

In your mouth there's much to do:
Bite, crunch, lick, blow, chew.
Engine changers can be dicey
If you like it sweet, or sour, or spicy.

Five ways, we've got five ways
To maximize your days.
Mouth, Move, Touch, Look, Listen
And find your way.

On the move, or on the go
No matter how fast or slow.
Front, back, circles, up or down
When your body craves it, just move around.
Heavy work is good for all
If your engine starts to stall.
If you find you're pumped or in a slump
It's OK to crash and bump.

Five ways, we've got five ways
To maximize your days.
Mouth, Move, Touch, Look, Listen
And find your way.

Touch is where some say
Fidgeting's now OK.
Click and tap and wiggle your pen
How good it feels when the rhythm kicks in.

TEST DRIVE: Introducing the Alert Program® Through Song

Five ways, we've got five ways
To maximize your days.
Mouth, Move, Touch, Look, Listen
And find your way.

With windows open wide
And all the shades drawn high.
When warm sunlight comes rushing in
It'll change that frown into a grin.

Five ways, we've got five ways
To maximize your days.
Mouth, Move, Touch, Look, Listen
And find your way.

If irritating sounds
Slow your progress down.
A squeaky chair, a dog that's barking
Time to get that engine sparking.
With music that calms your soul
Classic or rock and roll.
While some prefer to keep it quiet
Whatever it takes, make sure you try it!

Five ways, we've got five ways
To maximize your days.
Mouth, Move, Touch, Look, Listen
And find your way.

Five ways, we've got five ways
To maximize your days.
Five ways, we've got five ways!

Song Explanations and Suggestions: Five Ways Song

Five Ways
Song Explanation

BACKGROUND:

As we were "coming down the homestretch" in the recording studio and finishing the other songs for this CD, we felt that we needed one more song to explain further the Alert Program's® five ways to change engine levels. Sherry wrote the first draft of the lyrics to the Five Ways song early one morning. That afternoon, Don Wierman, a blues guitarist from Minneapolis, took the challenge to write the melody with improved lyrics (and he did it in record time). Together with the suggestions of Dennis Higgins, a musician and teacher of "twice exceptional" students, this song was "born."

Five Ways expands upon the Just Right Song's introduction to the engine analogy, the three levels of alertness, and the basic concept of how to change how alert one feels. Five Ways teaches students the five categories of engine strategies: put something in the mouth, move, touch, look, and listen. In addition, this song includes the characteristics of a "sensory diet," a term coined by Patricia Wilbarger, MA, OTR/L, FAOTA (1984), to describe our bodies' need for a sensory diet as well as a nutritional diet. Not all students are at a developmental age to learn these advanced Alert Program skills, but those who can, quickly widen their repertoire of engine strategies and learn what they can do to support their self-regulation when options are limited.

SIDE NOTE:

Dennis Higgins, teacher of "twice exceptional" students (those who are gifted with learning challenges) is quite exceptional himself as a musician and an educator for almost three decades.

For example, a child who finds chewing gum helpful while doing homework at home, may find it quite distressing to learn he is not allowed to chew gum at school. If he knows the characteristics of gum (it is in the mouth category, it is sweet, and it's chewy), then when options are limited, he has the skills to consider a replacement engine strategy such as raisins in his lunchbox (also in the mouth category, and raisins are sweet and chewy). If the school does not allow any food in classrooms for self-regulation, then the child can learn to choose a strategy from one of the other four ways to change engine levels (move, touch, look, or listen categories).

FIVE WAYS TO CHANGE ENGINE LEVELS:

Let's take a closer look at each of the five categories for changing engine levels. Five Ways offers examples that give students "the flavor" (no pun intended) of self-regulation strategies they can use to help keep their engine running just right.

PUT SOMETHING IN THE MOUTH:

As students sing the first verse, they learn *"In the mouth there's much to do: bite, crunch, lick, blow, chew...sweet, or sour, or spicy."* Patti Oetter, MA, OTR, FAOTA, was one of the first occupational therapists to understand the importance of the mouth and its effects on self-regulation, posture, and sensorimotor development (Oetter, Richter, & Frick, 1995; Frick, Frick, Oetter, & Richter, 1996).

Children can learn the characteristics of the mouth category by our discussing with them:

1) How does it feel? hard, soft, bumpy, smooth, slimy, cold, or hot

2) How does it taste? sweet, sour, salty, spicy, or bitter

2) What do you do with it? blow, suck, bite, crunch, chew, or lick

3) What food or non-food items can be used to change your engine in the mouth category? pretzels, gum, popcorn, bagels or whistles, straws, bubbles, or musical instruments.

MOVE:

In the move category, we teach children the following words to describe characteristics of motion: up/down, front/back, circles, upside down, heavy work, and crash/bump. Children usually catch on to the meaning of these words as we further explain that "heavy work" means activities that involve pushing, pulling, tugging, and towing such as pushing on a wall, carrying a heavy box, or playing tug of war. And we explain that the words "crash and bump" describe movements that are more intense than heavy work, such as jumping into a large pile of pillows, doing a "cannon ball" off of the diving board, or colliding in bumper cars.

In the second verse of the song, students learn, *"heavy work is good for all…"* because whether engines are in high or low, heavy work activities typically help engines return

SIDE NOTE:

Cindy Rodenbaugh, BS, fifth grade teacher in the Sonoma Country Day School, shares, "I had a particularly bright student who had difficulties with shouting and blurting out in class. He loved science and thought it was a great challenge and a lot of fun [to figure out which engine strategies helped him as a science experiment]. He chose a Sit-Fit (air-filled seating cushion). After about 45 minutes, he came up to me with a puzzled look on his face and said, 'I can't figure it out. When I'm sitting on this thing, I don't have the urge to blurt out!'…..What a great experiment!"

TEST DRIVE: Introducing the Alert Program® Through Song

Many of us find "touch" an important part of our sensory diet. Often we don't know how important touch is until we have a change in our daily routine. For example, once when we were lecturing in North Carolina, the hotel ran out of water and I (Mary Sue) was unable to take my typical hot shower that morning. I have some minor auditory processing and word finding issues that usually are not a problem, if my engine remains in an optimal state for teaching. I was quite surprised to discover how much more difficult it was for me to overcome my word finding problems while lecturing that day. Without my morning shower, my engine remained in low throughout the day, and my word finding problems were more challenging for me (and for the audience).

to just right. Although there are many ways to change engine levels, in the Alert Program we emphasize those that include heavy work because clinical observations show that it is rare for children to "overload" or become disorganized (engines going into really high gear) as a result of this type of movement. In summary, when offering movement strategies in the classroom or home, to avoid escalation and students' engines going into high, we recommend doing activities that involve heavy work. (*Take Five* contains more activity suggestions.)

TOUCH:

Singing the third verse, children learn, *"touch is where some say, fidgetin' is now OK."* Fidgeting can be misinterpreted as simply a sign of inattentiveness or even anxiousness. In fact, more often, in an attempt to remain alert, children, as well as adults, might fidget with anything handy: their jewelry, hair, cuticle, or paperclip while listening and attending. Many teachers have a desk drawer full of toys taken from children, only to find the same children who were fidgeting with these items bring in rocks from recess to fidget with! Some children focus better while fidgeting, others do get distracted. We suggest asking a comprehension question (while the child is holding the fidget toy) that the child typically can answer correctly. If the child can't answer correctly, then suggest another engine strategy to replace the fidget toy. But if the children can answer correctly, then we want to praise them for finding a good engine strategy.

For example, before a teacher reads a chapter of a Harry Potter book each day, she may pass out a basket of fidget toys or give each student a straw. After reading the chapter, the teacher can ask a question such as, "What happened after Harry knocked on the door?" If a student who typically can answer that type of question gives a blank stare or overly focuses on the fidget toy or straw, then the teacher can reply with a neutral tone of voice, "I don't think that fidget toy (or straw) worked to help your engine to listen to the story today. When I read again tomorrow, let's try having you sit on a camping pillow. That extra movement while you sit on the camping pillow might make it easier for you to stay in a just right engine level to listen to the story. OK?"

[Simplified Language Example: The teacher might not ask a direct question of a child who has language challenges. In the above example, the teacher will need to observe whether the strategy was working or not. She might notice that the fidget toy or straw is not supporting the child to listen to a simple story book. She might say to the child, "Oh, that is not helping. Try this pillow."]

SIDE NOTE:

"Camping pillows" are just one of many seating options that occupational therapists often recommend for students who need input in the move category to help their engines get to the just right speed for learning. A "Sit Fit" cushion is another air-filled seating option. For additional seating options, visit the websites of the companies listed in the Appendix.

LOOK:

The fourth verse gives examples of how visual input can change engine levels, *"with windows opened wide and all the shades drawn high"* or *"when warm sunlight comes rushing in, it'll change that frown into a grin."* Some children will relate more and understand better what they use in the look category by our talking with them about whether they like to read books, look at puzzles, or watch oil and water toys.

Further discussion can include preferences for variations in light (natural vs. artificial lighting), in types of colors (brightly painted rooms vs. soft pastels on walls), and in the amount of visual distractions (lots of posters on bedroom walls vs. blank walls). Often unconsciously, we adults choose environments that meet the visual needs of our sensory diet. For example, some people's engines would be in low all day if they lived in houses with dim lighting; others' engines might be fine, preferring the cozy feeling of such a cave-like home. Some need to live in sunny climates in houses with lots of bright natural lighting for their engines, while others prefer a rainy, cloudy climate.

LISTEN:

The last verse of **Five Ways** reminds us how much auditory input can affect our engines in positive or negative ways with the words, *"if irritating sounds, slow your progress down, a squeaky chair, a dog that's barking…* [and on the other hand] *music that calms your soul, classic, or rock and roll."* It is true that *"some prefer to keep it quiet,"* but quiet environments are becoming scarce these days with the increasing number of cell phones ringing, alarms sounding, and noises buzzing frequently throughout our environments. We recommend that children and their adults determine what things in the listen category support their engines. Characteristics include variables in volume (loud music vs. no music), in rhythm (rap music vs. Latin music), and in the amount of auditory distractions (studying at the library vs. a coffee shop).

In summary, many teachers, parents, and therapists using the Alert Program are surprised at how sophisticated students become when describing the characteristics of their engine needs (e.g., "I need something crunchy, spicy, and a little chewy right now to help me concentrate on my homework!"). Giving them vocabulary and a framework of categories to support their ability to change their level of alertness has resulted in students learning, as the song says, how to *"maximize their days."*

SIDE NOTE:

For an added challenge, after learning Five Ways, a classroom of students can be divided into five groups. Each group can be assigned one of the five ways (mouth, move, touch, look, and listen). When the class sings the chorus, each group can pop up to sing their word and then quickly sit back down again. The class will be popping up and down each time they hear their category of how to change engines. All can snap their fingers when they sing their word in the chorus: mouth (snap), move (snap), touch (snap), look (snap), listen (snap). Or they can do motions as they sing each of the words, such as: mouth (point to mouth), move (wiggle body), touch (grasp hands together), look (point to eyes), listen (point to ears).

TEST DRIVE: Introducing the Alert Program® Through Song

Engine Song

ENGINE SONG

Stop, think, what's my plan?
Make a good decision, yes I can.
I can run my engine on a speed that's just right.
Stop, think, what's my plan?

When I'm racing or cheering, jumping high in the sky,
Anyone can tell that my engine's on high.
I take quick breaths, my heart pumps fast,
I feel like I might never last.

What do you do?
Take a break (take a break)
Slow it down (slow it down)
Before I crash (before I crash)
Into the ground (into the ground).

Stop, think, what's my plan?
Make a good decision, yes I can.
I can run my engine on a speed that's just right.
Stop, think, what's my plan?

When I'm bored or feeling down,
I just mope and frown.
My engine's on low,
No energy head to toe.
My heart lubs slow,
I've got no go,
Can't hardly move,
No tae-kwon-do.

What do you do?
Call a friend (call a friend)
Hug a pet (hug a pet)
Munch a pickle (munch a pickle)
Don't forget (don't forget).

TEST DRIVE: Introducing the Alert Program® Through Song

Stop, think, what's my plan?
Make a good decision, yes I can.
I can run my engine on a speed that's just right.
Stop, think, what's my plan?

Playing fair with my friends,
Working hard at school,
Helping with a problem,
Keeping my cool.
I'm in charge of my engine speed.
Just right speed I'll go indeed.

How does it feel?
Feels good inside (good inside)
Filled with pride (filled with pride)
Friends and family (friends and family)
Side by side (side by side).

Stop, think, what's my plan?
Make a good decision, yes I can.
I can run my engine on a speed that's just right.
Stop, think, what's my plan?

Yes, I can run my engine on a speed that's just right.
Stop, think, what's my plan?

Song Explanations and Suggestions: Engine Song

Engine Song Explanation

BACKGROUND:

George Bednarczyk, a school psychologist in Winnipeg, Manitoba, wrote to us several years ago to explain an innovative way he was using the Alert Program® with his students. At the time, George was involved with several pilot prevention programs aimed at reducing conflict and violence in schools. He shared with us about his first experience in using the Alert Program with a group of three boys, whom he described as "in significant need of increasing their awareness and control of arousal states." George found not only that the boys "loved and looked forward to the sessions, they also were, in fact using the concepts with … success." One goal of the prevention program mandate was to incorporate whole-school interventions. To meet this goal, George knew that, in order for the Alert Program to be used school-wide, it needed a "hook." He and his team decided that a song could be that hook, and George created the **Engine Song**.

George later wrote,

> "The **Engine Song** has caught on at the whole school level. We use the song as an introduction to delivering segments of the Alert Program on a class-wide basis. Teachers have integrated the language of the Alert Program into their practice and they use techniques from the program on an ongoing basis to help their kids stay as

TEST DRIVE: Introducing the Alert Program® Through Song

'just right' as possible…(e.g., children keep their squeeze balls in their cubbies and bring them out if they need a fidget to help them stay just right). The song, coupled with home exercises, has integrated the ideas to families. And the song has been played at school assemblies and over the school intercom, as children enter their classrooms…The Engine Song has been a tremendously helpful vehicle for bringing the Alert Program to kids… and [I] wanted you to know how well the program has worked for us."

MY BONNIE LIES OVER THE OCEAN WARM-UP:

After George contacted TherapyWorks about his Engine Song, we had the good fortune to meet and watch George "in action," singing his song in front of more than 350 participants at an Alert Program adult training. As he does when working with his students, George started off singing My Bonnie Lies Over the Ocean as a warm up exercise. In campfire song tradition, he taught the audience the lively adaptation of the song by asking them to stand up when they heard a word starting with the letter "b" and then to sit down the next time they heard another word starting with the letter "b." In this way, the audience looked like popcorn, alternating between sitting and standing each time they heard a word beginning with the letter "b." It was quite a transformation to see all 350 audience members laughing and smiling and moving up and down to the music. After this warm up song, George had their attention and went on to teach the Engine Song. As with his students, the audience enthusiastically joined in singing the chorus: *"Stop, think, what's my plan? Make a good decision, yes I can. I can run my engine on a speed that's just right. Stop, think, what's my plan?"* George returned to Manitoba and later recorded the **Engine Song**. On the CD you can hear his students singing along with him, perhaps not even aware of how their adult friend successfully led an entire school to incorporate the Alert Program into their curriculum.

ENGINE SONG CHORUS AND VERSES:

In the **Engine Song**, you'll hear George singing the verses that portray the three engine levels with unique descriptions such as, *"My heart lubs slow, I've got no go. Can't hardly move, no tae kwon do."* After each verse, George sings the question, *"What do you do?"* Then George sings examples of engine strategies, and the children eagerly echo the answers. They learn through the playful words of the song that they can be in charge of their engine speed as they explore a variety of ways to change their level of alertness.

George wrote the **Engine Song** to combine the Alert Program with other self-control programs his school was using with their students (Borba, 2001; Whitehouse & Pudney, 1996). Also, the **Engine Song** adds the social-emotional aspects of self-regulation with phrases such as, *"Playing fair with my friends"* or *"helping with a problem."* In response to the questions, *"What do you do?"* the children respond, *"Call a friend"* or *"hug a pet."* And in the final verse when asked, *"How does it feel?"*, the children sing the refrain, *"Feels good inside, filled with pride, friends and family, side by side."* These relational components of the **Engine**

SIDE NOTE

Another unique part of the approach at George's school was the work done with the speech and language pathologist, Sharon Halldorson. They included Alert Program concepts in her classroom-based work on phonemic awareness (analyzing the sounds of language and how these sounds make up words and sentences). One clever collaboration was a story/ poem ("Don't Forget to Get a Pet"), which was a tale of two siblings who had been promised a visit to the pet shop to get a new family pet. The "plot" involved the siblings going through their day and working to keep their engines running just right. This is a great example of how more "traditional" curriculum goals can easily incorporate self-regulation themes.

TEST DRIVE: Introducing the Alert Program® Through Song

Song expand upon the basics of the Alert Program to encompass the needs of all children to be appreciated, to be liked, and to feel part of a group.

We hope you will enjoy singing the **Engine Song** with your students as much as we have. It is a wonderful way to teach a myriad of concepts such as fostering impulse control, the need for cooperation, and the importance of being a friend. You may want to discuss the lines of the song in more detail with your students. In this way, you can initiate a discussion to further explain that, *"I can run my engine on a speed that's just right…* [and I can] *Stop, think, what's my plan?"*

ADDITIONAL SONGS WITH MOTION

Singing songs with motions is an excellent engine strategy. Remember that breath supports self-regulation. For example, we know that quick, shallow breathing (upper chest breathing) is common when our engines are in high, and a traditional relaxation technique is to encourage deep, belly breathing (diaphragmatic breathing).

Here's a partial list of camp-type songs with motions that can be used with elementary-aged students in classroom, home, or therapy settings. Many early childhood educators use songs that incorporate motions in preschool and kindergarten; we hope this list sparks other titles that you can use with the older students in your setting. You can easily search more on the Internet, but here's a beginning list:

Alive, Awake, Alert, Enthusiastic
www.scoutingaround.com

Banana Dance
www.scoutingaround.com

Bear Hunt
www.dltk-kids.com

Bingo
www.scoutingaround.com

BoogaLoo Song
www.boyscouttrail.com

Chester
www.scoutingaround.com

Do Your Ears Hang Low?
www.scoutingaround.com

Grand Old Duke of York
www.scoutingaround.com

Have You Ever Been Fishing?
www.drjean.org

Head, Shoulders, Knees and Toes
www.scoutingaround.com

Hello, Neighbor!
www.drjean.org

Hokey Pokey
www.scoutingaround.com

Hokey Pokey Animal Version
www.jackhartmann.com

Macarena
www.en.wikipedia.org

My Bonnie Lies over the Ocean
www.scoutingaround.com

One Finger, One Thumb
www.scoutingaround.com

Take Me Out to the Ball Game
www.kididdles.com

Wally Acha
www.drjean.org

YMCA dance motions
www.en.wikipedia.org

Alive, Awake
Alert Song

ALIVE, AWAKE, ALERT

(Sung to **If You're Happy and You Know It** with motions similar to **Head, Shoulders, Knees and Toes**)

I'm Alive, [touch toes]
Awake, [touch knees]
Alert, [touch shoulders]
Enthusiastic [arms spread wide reaching for the sky]

I'm Alive, [touch toes]
Awake, [touch knees]
Alert, [touch shoulders]
Enthusiastic [arms spread wide reaching for the sky]

Alive, [touch toes]
Awake, [touch knees]
Alert, [touch shoulders]

Alert, [touch shoulders]
Awake, [touch knees]
Alive, [touch toes]

Alive, [touch toes]
Awake, [touch knees]
Alert, [touch shoulders]
Enthusiastic [arms spread wide reaching for the sky]

TEST DRIVE: Introducing the Alert Program® Through Song

Alive, Awake, Alert
Song Explanation

BACKGROUND:

We first sang the Alive, Awake, Alert song around a campfire, along with some 50 campers with special needs at Camp Avanti (mentioned earlier). We knew this song would become one of our favorites as we watched the campers' faces light up with smiles and heard the giggles and laughter, and as we all attempted to keep up with the increasing speed of the music. We have used this song with children and adults alike as a movement break, when engines are in non-optimal alert levels in schools, homes, or therapy settings. The song never fails to elicit smiles, giggles, and laughter, as well as supporting self-regulation.

In addition to improving self-regulation, teachers, parents, and therapists will find many other advantages to singing this song. The challenge is trying to do the motions faster and faster. The song requires timing and sequencing of movements. While children are concentrating on the motions of the song, they are using motor planning and body awareness skills. Gross motor coordination and a quick cardiovascular workout are additional benefits.

PERIODS OF MOVEMENT FOLLOWED BY PERIODS OF CONCENTRATION:

To provide a movement break, teachers can ask students to sing this song between subjects, such as, "Boys and girls, let's get our bodies and brains ready for math. Let's sing **Alive, Awake, Alert**. Ready?" In this way, the song's movements can support children to obtain an optimal state for learning the new math concepts.

As adults, we create these types of movement breaks often, and usually automatically, throughout our day. A secretary's job may require a lot of typing while sitting at a desk in a small office or cubicle. Rarely would a person type from 9 am to 12 noon without taking a stretch break or walking to the lounge for a cup of coffee. Much research has been done on ergonomics and the best ways to avoid injuries to our bodies through proper positioning and movement breaks (Jacobs, 1999), but these movement breaks also help us to self-regulate, therefore, to concentrate and focus better.

Preschool teachers understand the concept of "periods of movement followed by periods of concentration" completely. They would never dream of asking a child to sit in circle time for two hours! They would expect behavior problems if they did such a thing. Instead, preschool teachers understand that providing periods of movement, such as walking like elephants or jumping like bunnies to circle time, helps the body prepare to sit for a short period of time. Then after a few minutes of concentration, perhaps talking about the day's weather and naming the day of the week, the teacher helps the children sing a song that

TEST DRIVE: Introducing the Alert Program® Through Song

involves motions or marching to music. A preschooler's day is filled with alternating periods of movement followed by periods of concentration.

Older children need the same type of self-regulation support, but for some reason it is less common to see frequent movement breaks in the later grades. Children have different "formulas" of how much movement is needed at what level of intensity, frequency, or duration, in order to attain a just right engine level for learning or playing (Oetter, 1991). For one child five minutes of marching to music may help the nervous system to then focus on reading for 20 minutes. Later, the child may need another two minutes of heavy work in order to concentrate again. For another child, three minutes of isometrics may be the best engine strategy to gain 25 minutes of focus for reading. Then again, a child with more severe sensory challenges may need five minutes of playing tug of war with an adult to gain five minutes of focus. Even so, this may end up being less disruptive than the time needed to manage behavior problems or to risk the child not feeling successful.

SONG LYRICS AND MOTION VARIATIONS:

The lyrics of Alive, Awake, Alert are sung to the tune, If You're Happy and You Know It with motions that are similar to Head, Shoulders, Knees, and Toes. Many variations on both the lyrics and the motions can be found on the Internet. We prefer the motions of first touching the toes, then knees, then shoulders, and ending with arms stretched toward the sky (while singing *"enthusiastically"*).

On the *Test Drive* CD, you will hear **Alive, Awake, Alert** is repeated five times. Explain to the students that the pace will increase, making the motions more and more challenging each time the song is sung. As the tempo increases, children receive vestibular input, involving the part of the brain that makes sense out of movement and gravity. Occasionally this type of movement can contribute to a child's engine going up into high gear. If this happens, it may be an indication of the need for more heavy work or other sensory input than this song can provide. Encourage the child to jump, push on a wall, or get a deep bear hug; these types of deep touch and heavy work movement usually will help engines return to an optimal state for learning. (If these simple heavywork strategies do not help, consult an occupational therapist for other options and to better understand the child's nervous system. See Children with Special Needs section.)

Other motion variations include the following:

VARIATION #1
Alive [slap hands on thighs]
Awake [clap hands once]
Alert [snap fingers once]
Enthusiastic [put arms in air and do the "Twist"]

VARIATION #2
I'm alive [hands on head]
Alert [hands on shoulders]
Awake [hands crossed on chest]
Enthus- [slap thighs]
Ias- [clap hands]
Tic [click fingers of both hands]

TEST DRIVE: Introducing the Alert Program® Through Song

VARIATION #3

This variation is included in an excellent downloadable resource called *Pathways: Exercise Breaks* (Davis, 1999). In this version of the song, students are divided into three groups while seated at their desks. The first group stands and sits back down when the word *"Alive"* is sung, the second group when the word *"Awake"* is sung, and the third group when the word *"Alert"* is sung. All stand and sit back down when the word *"Enthusiastic"* is sung. It is suggested that the teacher writes the words on the chalkboard so students know when to stand (especially for those who learn best with visual cues).

VARIATION #4

We came across another variation for the lyrics that may be appropriate only for older students who can enjoy such unique humor. Obviously, these words would be inappropriate for those in primary grades or those who would be offended by the words. In campfire tradition, however, some children at certain ages enjoy "playing" with such words that are "on the edge." The song is sung in a similar way with your choice of motions:

I'm dead, asleep, lethargic and unconscious
I'm dead, asleep, lethargic and unconscious
I'm dead, asleep, lethargic
Lethargic, dead, asleep
I'm dead, asleep, lethargic, and unconscious.

VARIATION #5

You might want to encourage children to write their own lyrics to the song to describe their engine levels. A teacher could have the whole class contribute words to write new lyrics as a group to describe the three different engine levels. For example, the song could have three verses, one for each engine level, with words such as:

Engine's on high, wild, and hyped out
Engine's on high, wild, and hyped out
High, wild, hyped out
Hyped out, wild, and high.
Engine's on high, wild, and hyped out.

Engine's in low, droopy, feeling slow
Engine's in low, droopy, feeling slow
Low, droopy, feeling slow
Feeling slow, droopy, and low
Engine's in low, droopy, feeling slow.

Engine's Just Right, alert, and focused.
Engine's Just Right, alert, and focused.
Just Right, alert, and focused.
Focused, alert and Just Right.
Engine's Just Right, alert, and focused.

VARIATION #6

And for one last variation, by singing the same melody and changing a few words of If You're Happy and You Know It, you have a song that can be used to bring groups back together. Teachers can sing the following lyrics to the song, for example, after recess, when they want students to return to their seats, focused and ready to learn. Or before giving a spelling test, a teacher might sing this version of the song to prepare students' engines for the test. We sing it at our Alert Program® trainings when we want the participants to return to their seats after a snack break.

In addition to bringing groups back together, this song supports children to obtain a just right engine gear for a task or activity. A parent might sing it to a child to help her wake up and become alert in the morning. (The child might start singing the song, even attempting the motions while still in the bed). Or a therapist may sing the song before giving instructions and starting a therapy session to be sure the child is in an optimal state for learning.

Mary Sue "rearranged" the words and motions for this version:

If you're ready and you know it,
Clap your hands [Clap hands twice]
If you're ready and you know it,
Stomp your feet [Stomp feet twice]
If you're ready and you know it,
Then your engine will surely show it
If you're ready and you know it,
Clap your hands [Clap hands twice]
Stomp your feet [Stomp feet twice]

Say, "I'm ready!"
"I'm ready!"

Whether working with large groups or one-on-one, with adolescents or young children, you will find that **Alive, Awake, Alert** (and its many variations) supports engines in a joyful and effective manner. Experiment with your students and discover what version of the song they enjoy most.

SIDE NOTE:

Carla Cay Williams, OT/L, our international Alert Program trainer, shares her experience with a nine-year-old boy who she treats at her therapy clinic, KidPower Therapy Associates. This child-we'll call him Juan-is overly sensitive to touch, sounds, food tastes, and textures. He has difficulty taking in and making sense of movement and gravity. And he has severe challenges in understanding others verbally and expressing himself. All of these problems become worse when Juan's engine drops into low gear.

This Alive, Awake, Alert *song might not be the best pick for Juan's nervous system for several reasons. Juan tends to be reluctant to move when his engine is in low. Because* Alive, Awake, Alert *doesn't include heavy work (intensity) and with his sensitivities to sounds, Juan's engine might go from low, miss the just right speed, and end up in high gear. However, he's not hyperactive, as one might expect. When his engine is in high gear, he shows more intense emotions. He might "melt into a puddle" on the floor, but then quickly he can begin to scream, cry, kick, and even knock over furniture. You can well imagine that Juan, his parents, and his teachers want to avoid that kind of scene.*

As Juan learns about his engine, Carla and his family report he has made good strides in beginning to understand what he can do to change how alert he feels. He still needs guidance and is encouraged to talk about how his engine is doing. Juan is learning to change his engine levels so it becomes easier for him to interact with his friends and family. (See Children with Special Needs section.)

Transition
Songs

Transition Songs Explanation

Times of transition can be quite challenging, especially to the child who has difficulty with taking in and making sense of what they hear, see, touch, taste, or smell. If you know a child who has trouble ending one activity and beginning another activity or moving from one part of the school or home (the classroom or garage) to another part of the school or home (lunchroom or kitchen), you may want to try using one of the **Transition Songs**. There can be many reasons for difficulties in transitions, but this is one possible way to make these times of the day easier for children.

We recorded some of the *Test Drive* songs without lyrics to create the final four tracks of the CD. (Each track varies in duration: 30 seconds, one minute, two minutes, and three minutes long.) These tracks can be used to support engines in times of transition in classrooms, homes, and therapy settings.

BACKGROUND:

Barbara Piper, MA, works in the Albuquerque Public Schools as a special education teacher and behavior consultant. After listening to **Best Work**, she suggests playing…

> "the songs as part of an auditory cue for transition between learning tasks or as a transition between classroom events. The teacher can tell the students

SIDE NOTE:

Nina Araújo, co-author of Easy Songs for Smooth Transitions (Araujo & Aghayan, 2006) explains,

"In a classroom, a transition is the time between two activities or routines during the day; for example, the time between free choice and circle time or between snack and outdoor play. On average, in a full-day, group-care program, children and adults experience between sixteen and twenty transitions daily. At five to ten minutes per transition, up to three hours are spent in this manner each day. Transitions represent change—change in activity, energy level, space, and/or focus. Change is difficult for all of us, but especially for young children. Transitions also offer great learning opportunities. Children can learn about prediction, difference, problem solving, inclusion, and how to smoothly and playfully shift focus" (Araújo, 2006).

TEST DRIVE: Introducing the Alert Program® Through Song

that he will play one of the transition songs and by the end of the song, the students need to have put their materials away and be in their seats" (personal communication, May 2006).

We appreciate her idea that enhances classroom management based on an understanding of engine levels.

HOW TO USE THE TRANSITION SONGS:

Teachers, parents, or therapists can choose whether to play the track that is 30 seconds, one minute, two minutes, or three minutes in duration, depending on the length of time that is needed to prepare for the next activity. For example, as students are finishing their silent reading, the teacher might say, "Let's get ready for our math lesson. I'm going to play the 30 Second Song. By the end of the song, I want you to put your books away, find your math book, and open it to page 42. Ready?" Then the teacher plays the 30 second track and the students move about as they prepare for their math lesson. To ensure success for the visual learners in the classroom, the teacher might write the directions on the chalkboard, such as, "Math book, page 42."

[Simplified Language Example: For a child who has speech and language challenges, the teacher might say, "30 Second Song! Put books in desks, sit to get ready, go!"]

As children become accustomed to using music in this way, teachers find how much easier they transition from one activity to another throughout their school day with fewer behavioral problems. If familiar with the Alert

Program® concepts, children can be encouraged, while listening to the Transition Songs, to choose an engine strategy that will get them to a just right alert level for the next activity.

For example, children who have completed the Alert Program would be able to follow the teacher's instructions, "You have been doing an excellent job concentrating on our history lesson this morning. Let's all check in with our engines and think about what type of movement we need to get to a just right level. We're going to be talking about our new science project next, and I want us all to be in the best place for learning. My engine is in low right now and I need to do some jumping. Think about what your engine needs and I'm going to play the One Minute Song. Move any way that feels good to your engine while you listen to the song. When the song is over, I want everyone back in their seats and ready to start our science lesson." Then the teacher plays the One Minute Song, and all the children jump, dance, do isometrics, push on a wall, or move their bodies in any way that supports their engines.

When the song stops, the teacher could comment, "I really liked how you made good choices and were safe in the ways you were moving. Jumping helped my engine and I feel ready to focus on science now. Anybody still need some help to get their engine to just right for our science lesson?" Then the teacher could remind the students about the five ways to change engine levels and help the individual students choose a strategy to get into a just right gear for focusing on science.

SIDE NOTE:

If children are developmentally not at an age where they can understand these advanced Alert Program skills, the Transition Songs may not be appropriate. These children's caregivers and teachers can use visual schedule cues, timers (auditory or visual), and other means of signaling the length of an activity (when to begin and stop). As we know, many children need a lot of structure, and others do better with less structure. Some respond best to predictable schedules, and others "go with the flow" more easily. Therefore, respect for these preferences is needed, along with a willingness to continue to experiment and observe what is most supportive.

TEST DRIVE: Introducing the Alert Program® Through Song

Obviously, students need to be familiar with the Alert Program and to have experimented with ways to change engine levels (Stage Two in the *Leader's Guide*) before they would be expected to be independent in this type of self-regulation. We would not expect students to do this without first learning in Stage One, how to label their engine levels; in Stage Two, how to begin choosing engine strategies; and in Stage Three, to be guided to understand their own sensory diet needs.

Also, notice in this example that the teacher first describes her own engine level to the students and shares what engine strategy she is going to use. This helps to reinforce students' thinking about their engine levels and making good engine strategy choices.

VARIOUS USES FOR THE TRANSITION SONGS:

We used the classroom environment as an example of how to utilize the Transition Songs, but this could be easily adapted for times of transition in home or therapy settings. For example, a parent might play the Transition Songs to help a youngster prepare to dress himself in the morning. After the child awakens and perhaps brushes his teeth or eats breakfast, the parent might say, "Let's get dressed and ready for our day. I'm going to play the 30 Second Song. By the end of the song, I want you in your bedroom. I'll meet you there to help you get dressed." Likewise, an occupational therapist in a clinic might say at the end of therapy session, "Boy, we sure had fun today. It's time to stop and go meet your mom in the waiting room. Sometimes it's hard to stop playing, so I'm going to play the One Minute Song. When the song stops, I want you to be at the door and then we'll go tell your mom all the fun things we did today."

Another variation on the use of music in times of transition is offered by Kate Andrews, a teacher in Orlando, FL:

> "Between subjects, or when you want the students to transition to another subject, play a particular song. In the beginning of the year, allow the students to choose what songs they would like to hear for a particular subject. For example, math might be **Somewhere Over the Rainbow**, reading might be [This Land is Your Land]... When the students hear that song being played, they know that it is time to clean up and transition to the next subject. The students have until the end of the song to be completely ready. As a teacher you will have to decide what completely 'ready' is. For example, pencil, paper and next subject book out, everything put away and their hands on the table, etc." (Andrews, 2005).

Building upon Kate's suggestion, you might want to choose different songs from the *Test Drive* CD. Playing the same song at the same time each day offers students predictability and stability to cope with transitions. One preschool teacher uses a John Philip Sousa march and encourages cleanup each day with a "pick-up parade." Using the **Transition Songs** or other music is just one way to support children through times of transition. There are many other resources available. Ask your occupational therapist, behavior specialist, or other professionals for suggestions; a vast array of treatment modalities may be appropriate for students who have significant problems with transitions. The use of Transition Songs is just one more tool in your "tool box of options" for supporting children.

Song Explanations and Suggestions: Transition Songs

As You Begin to "Test Drive" the Alert Program

Children With Special Needs: Handle With Care

As teachers, parents, and therapists we all try to do our very best to support children and keep them safe. As authors, we've made recommendations in this book that will guide you to introduce the Alert Program® through song. Please continue to use your professional (and parental) judgment when choosing which songs and activities are most appropriate for the children you are working and living with, especially those with special needs such as the physically, visually, hearing, or mentally challenged and medically fragile. In closing, we want to mention one additional exceptionality. The following excerpt is taken from *Take Five* in describing those with "sensory defensiveness":

Children who experience the world as unsafe, alarming, or irritating due to the way in which their brains misinterpret the sensory input in their environments may have sensory defensiveness. One of the brain's main jobs is to protect the body.

> "Sensory defensiveness is simply the overactivation of our protective senses. It is a misperception that makes our clothes feel like spiders on our skin and stairs seem like cliffs. . . . Common symptoms may include over sensitivity to light or unexpected touch, sudden movement or over reaction to unstable surfaces, high frequency noises, excesses of noise or visual stimuli, and certain smells" (Wilbarger & Wilbarger, 1991, p. 1).

Normally developing children experience the "joyful exploration of sensation" (Wilbarger, 1991-2006). Some children are more cautious than others, but when children seem fearful, especially in new situations, in times of transition, or when exploring new materials, we want to rule out the possibility of an underlying problem. Professionals trained in sensory processing theory and treatment can identify possible causes. Some children require occupational therapy or other professional help to address their needs and help them feel "comfort, safety, confidence, and competence" (Oetter, 1983).

Any nervous system will respond to protect the body if the brain's perception is that of danger. To an observer, this reaction may seem extreme, but the brain's first priority is protection of the body. Therefore, a real threat or perceived threat (based on past or present experience) is handled in the same way. A perceived threat is real to the perceiver, and it needs to be honored as her truth. As parents and teachers, we must honor children's perception of their sensorimotor world and respect their needs.

Children who are sensory defensive cannot be "desensitized" by being forced to participate in activities that their nervous system perceives as dangerous or irritating. These children need our understanding and support. Their engines quickly can go into high gear and sometimes go over the edge when their brains try to shut out the sensory bombardment completely; their engines may look like they are in a low level of alertness (engine in low gear), when truly their nervous systems are shut down.

This is a serious condition of the nervous system. Children who have sensory defensiveness can rapidly go into this shutdown state.

Watch for symptoms of sensory defensiveness. If you observe this type of reaction to any sensory input (from what they see, feel, taste, touch, smell, or certain types of movement), ask an occupational therapist or other professional trained in sensory processing theory and treatment for an evaluation and recommendations. Occupational therapists can treat sensory defensiveness with intensive therapies to remediate the underlying problem.

If you observe children having any type of difficulty with sensorimotor activities or you are concerned for a child's safety, stop the activity and seek consultation from another professional. As with any advice or suggestions regarding children, it is the adults' responsibility to provide a safe, properly supervised environment. Of course, TherapyWorks, Inc. cannot be responsible for negligent or improper use of suggestions made in *Test Drive*, but we all should "handle children with care." All children are special and deserve our gentle, loving care so they will flourish and grow to share their unique gifts with the world.

Our Final Thoughts...

Our goal in creating this *Test Drive* book and CD is to provide an easy and practical way to share information about self-regulation in school, home, or therapy settings. The "test drive" title is cute, but we really want you to take the Alert Program® out for a spin. Help others take it for a spin and see what they think. If you are new to the Alert Program, these songs and related suggestions are designed to provide the essentials to get you started. If you have prior experience with the Alert Program, *Test Drive* reinforces your ability to help others understand the importance of self-regulation in achieving educational or therapeutic goals.

Good luck as you begin "introducing the Alert Program through song"! We welcome hearing the creative ways that our readers adapt and implement the Alert Program. Your experiences with your students, clients, sons, or daughters can help us all learn more about self-regulation. Care to share an uplifting anecdote, unusual adaptation, new engine vocabulary, successful self-regulation strategy, or an "ah-ha" moment? Go to www.AlertProgram.com to share your story.

Ready, get set, start your engines! Go ahead…take it out for a spin and "test drive" the Alert Program through song!

REFERENCES

REFERENCES

Andrews, Kate (2005). Classroom management. Retrieved August 22, 2006, from Classroom Management Web site: http://66.102.7.104/search?q=cache:g3p1e5klBSgJ:www.kdp.org/forms/assets/work/classroom%20management%20techniques.doc+kate+Andrews+transition+songs&hl=en&gl=us&ct=clnk&cd=1

Araújo, N., & Aghaya, C. (2006). *Easy songs for smooth transitions in the classroom*. St. Paul: Red Leaf.

Araújo, N. (2006). Daily transitions and participatory songs. Retrieved August 22, 2006, from Red Leaf Press Web site: http://redleafpress.org/client/archives/features/rl_Jun2006_feature.cfm

Ayres, A. J. (1979). *Sensory integration and the child*. Los Angeles: Western Psychological Services.

Borba, M. (2001). *Building moral intelligence: The seven essential virtues that teach kids to do the right thing*. San Francisco: Jossey Bass.

Davis, S. M. (1999). Welcome to Pathways. Retrieved August 26, 2006, from Pathways Web site: http://hsc.unm.edu/pathways

Frick, S., Frick, R., Oetter, P., & Richter, E. (1996). *Out of the mouth of babes: Discovering the developmental significance of the mouth*. Hugo, MN: Professional Development Programs.

Hallowell, E. (2006). *Crazy busy overstretched, overbooked and about to snap: Strategies for coping in a world gone ADD*. New York: Random House.

Jacobs, K. (Ed.). (1999). *Ergonomics for therapists*. (2nd ed.) New York City: Butterworth-Heinneman.

Koomar, J. (2003). What is sensory integration? Retrieved August 25, 2006, from Occupational Therapy Associates – Watertown, P.C. Web site: http://www.otawatertown.com/sensory.html

Lane, S. (2002). Sensory Modulation. In A.C. Bundy, S.J. Lane, & E.A. *Murray, Sensory integration: Theory and practice.* (2nd ed.) (pp.101-122). Philadelphia: F.A. Davis.

Miller, L. J., Cermak, S., Lane, S., Anzalone, M., & Koomar, J. (Summer 2004). Position statement on terminology related to sensory integration dysfunction. *S.I. Focus*, 6-8.

Miller, L. J. (2006). Frequently Asked Questions. Retrieved August 25, 2006, from Kid Foundation Web site: http://www.spdnetwork.org/faq/index.html

Oetter, P. (1991). Sensorimotor planning worksheet. In M.S. Williams & S. Shellenberger (Eds.), *"How does your engine run?" A leader's guide to the alert program for self-regulation.* (p. 1-14). Albuquerque, NM: TherapyWorks.

Oetter, P. (1983). Sensory integration treatment course. Paper presented for Professional Development Programs, multiple locations.

Oetter, P., Richter, E., & Frick, S. (1995). *MORE: Integrating the mouth with sensory and postural functions.* Hugo, MN: Professional Development Programs.

Rotz, R., & Wright, S. (2005). *Fidget to focus.* Lincoln, NE: iUniverse.

Salls, J., & Bucey, J. (2003). Self-regulation strategies for middle school students. *OT Practice*, 8, 11-16.

SII (1991). *Caution: Children at Work*, The Ayres Clinic at Sensory Integration International (poster). Torrance, CA.

Whitehouse, E., & Pudney, W. (1996). *A volcano in my tummy: Helping children to handle anger.* Gabriola Island, BC, Canada: New Society.

Wilbarger, P. (1984). Planning an adequate sensory diet: Application of sensory processing theory during the first year of life. *Zero to Three*, V(1), 7-12.

Wilbarger, P., & Wilbarger, J. (1991). *Sensory defensiveness in children aged 2-12: An intervention guide for parents and other caregivers.* Santa Barbara, CA: Avanti Educational Programs.

Wilkinson, L., Scholey, A., Wesnes, K. (2002). Chewing gum selectively improves aspects of memory in healthy volunteers. *Appetite* 38, 235-236.

Williams, M. S., & Shellenberger, S. A. (1996). *"How does your engine run?" A leader's guide to the alert program for self-regulation.* Albuquerque, NM: TherapyWorks.

Williams, M. S., & Shellenberger, S. A. (2001). *Take Five! Staying alert at home and school.* Albuquerque, NM: TherapyWorks.

TEST DRIVE: Introducing the Alert Program® Through Song

APPENDIX

Additional Resources

American Occupational Therapy Association
www.aota.org

Brain Gym International
www.braingym.org

Child Development Media, Inc.
www.childdevelopmentmedia.com

Developmental Delay Resources
www.devdelay.org

**Developmental FX The Developmental &
Fragile X Resource Centre**
www.developmentalfx.org

Hallowell Center
www.drhallowell.com

Handwriting without Tears
www.hwtears.com

Harcourt Assessment
www.harcourtassessment.com

Henry Occupational Therapy Services
www.henryot.com

Integrations
www.integrationscatalog.com

Learning Disabilities Association of America
www.ldanatl.org

Occupational Therapy Associates–Watertown, P.C.
www.otawatertown.com

Oriental Trading Company
www.orientaltrading.com

Out-of-Sync Child
www.out-of-sync-child.com

Pocket Full of Therapy
www.pfot.com

TEST DRIVE: Introducing the Alert Program® Through Song

Professional Development Programs
  www.pdppro.com

REI
  www.rei.com

Sammons Preston Roylan
  www.sammonspreston.com

Sensory Integration UK & Ireland
  www.sensoryintegration.org.uk

Sensory Processing Disorder Foundation
  www.spdfoundation.net

Sensory Tools
  www.sensorytools.net

SouthPaw Enterprises
  www.southpawenterprises.com

TEACCH Autism Program
  www.teacch.com

The Gray Center for Social Learning and Understanding
  www.thegraycenter.org

Therapro
  www.theraproducts.com

Vital Links
  www.vitallinks.net

Weighted Wearables
  www.weightedwearables.com

Western Psychological Services
  www.wpspublish.com

To: School Staff
From: Mary Sue Williams and Sherry Shellenberger
RE: Singing the "Just Right Song" in Your Upcoming Assembly

We are pleased to have the opportunity to meet weekly with your colleague, Dennis Higgins, to create some new songs for children based on the Alert Program. The book, *How Does Your Engine Run?® A Leader's Guide to the Alert Program® for Self-Regulation (Williams & Shellenberger, 1996)*, describes this program that supports children, teachers, parents, and therapists to choose appropriate strategies to change or maintain states of alertness. Students learn what they can do before a spelling test or homework time to attain an optimal state of alertness for their tasks. Teachers learn what they can do after lunch, when their adult nervous systems are in a low alert state and their students are in a high alert state. Parents learn what they can do to help their child's nervous system change from a high alert state to a more appropriate low state at bedtime.

We are occupational therapists who believe that all of us (children and adults, typically and not so typically developing) can benefit from understanding how we change how alert we feel throughout our day. We share with children, "If your body is like a car engine, sometimes it runs on high, sometimes it runs on low, and sometimes it runs just right." Using this simple engine analogy, students (and their adults) learn five ways to change engine levels: put something in your mouth, move, touch, look, and listen.

We heard from Dennis that your school currently is administering standardized testing. We are always looking for ways to learn more from students, whom we consider to be our "finest teachers." We will be with Dennis in your afternoon assembly next week to teach a song to your student body about the five ways they can use to change how alert they feel. We hope the song will be helpful to you and your students' engines for what can be quite stressful days of testing.

The song will introduce your students to what it might look like when their engines are in high (hyper, wild, out of control), in low (feeling lethargic or like a "couch potato"), or just right (alert, focused, and attentive). Also, the song will teach your students the five ways to change engine levels. All of us use things from the mouth, move, touch, look, and listen categories in order to help us focus and concentrate.

Think about the "old days," when we used to talk on phones with cords. What did we do when the conversations lasted more than a few minutes?

• We would put a pencil to our mouth to chew on (mouth category),
• pace the few feet back and forth as allowed by the cord (move category),
• we would twirl the cord with our fingers (touch category), or
• we would doodle on the phone book or nearby piece of paper (look category)

TEST DRIVE: Introducing the Alert Program® Through Song

- We would do all of these things to try to give our brain what it needed to concentrate in the phone conversation (listen category).

To help students' engines get to the just right state for doing their best on the standardized testing, you might want to encourage students to do activities that involve heavy work because heavy work "works" when engines are in high or low to get to the just right level. In general, to avoid escalation and students' engines going into high, we recommend doing activities that involve heavy work. Heavy work to muscles and joints stimulates the inner part of the brain. This stimulation tells the brain, "Chill out... calm down... we can relax and focus." Each day before starting the testing or between subtests you might have your students:

- **march to music**
- **sing a song while pushing on a wall or on their desktops**
- **do chair push-ups**
  1) Place arms on either side of the chair.
  2) Scoot bottom away from the back of the chair.
  3) Try to straighten arms, lifting bottom off of the chair.

- **do isometrics**
  1) Place palms together and push for five seconds.
  2) Then relax for a few seconds and repeat two to five times.
  3) Next, curl the fingers on each hand to form a semicircle. Rotate one hand toward the body and one hand way from the body. Interlock your fingers, imitating a position of singing opera. Pull your elbows in opposite directions. Relax and repeat.
  4) In the same manner (holding a position and then relaxing), raise both hands to reach for the ceiling. Then shrug shoulders up toward ears. Finally place right palm on right knee. Push up with the knee and down with the hand. Hold and repeat with left hand and knee, as with all other positions listed above.

- **use a straw** (tug/pull/chew/bite on it or bend it with the hand)
  NOTE: Gum is an excellent way to get heavy work to the jaw joint, but it is often not allowed in classrooms. So if gum is not allowed, we suggest a straw for both the mouth and/or touch categories.

  Of course, you can set up rules, such as "you abuse, it you lose it"! You might be surprised how a simple straw can support "engines."

**WE LOOK FORWARD TO SINGING WITH YOUR STUDENTS
AND BEST TO YOU (AND YOUR ENGINE)
FOR THE STANDARIZED TESTING!**

To: School Staff
From: Mary Sue Williams and Sherry Shellenberger
RE: Song Lyrics and Straws for Classroom

We will be in the assembly this afternoon, excited to try out our new Just Right Song with you and your students (lyrics attached). As we mentioned in the letter at the end of last week, we'll be teaching your students a song about what they can do when they are having trouble concentrating, learning, or doing their best on the standardized tests this week. "Using a straw" will be in the song as one of the ways to help students to keep their engines running "just right." Here are some straws that you can use after we teach the song, if you'd like to support students while completing their standardized testing. A supply will be in your box each day this week, so if they are lost, displaced, or confusion arise about whose straw is whose, no problem! Please consider them totally disposable.

Before we give straws to students, we find it helpful to ask them what classroom rules we might need. Your students will learn in the song that chewing on a straw can be "brain food for the mouth" or bending the neck of the straw can be a "brain toy" for the hand. We usually explain to students something like, "You might be surprised that a straw can actually help you to concentrate. Here are some straws for you to use... (be sure to allow students a few minutes to explore and experiment with the straw to allow the "novelty" to wear off before expecting them to use them as "brain food" or "brain toys")..."In the song, we learned that straws can help our engines to run 'just right' to make school easier. Let's try out the straws and see if they help our engines. What will it look like if you are using the straws to help your engine?.... What are things we should not do with our straws? ...." Then after the discussion, we usually summarize with a statement such as: "If you are not being safe with the straws by respecting yourself, others, or the environment, you'll have to toss it away for today."

As we mentioned last week in our note, many of us used to pay attention in long phone conversations (on the old phones with cords) by putting a pen to our mouth or twirling the phone cord. Similarly, your students may chew on the straw, bend the neck of the straw back and forth, or tie a knot in the straw, etc. to help them pay attention. If a student appears to be so focused on the straw and is not able to answer questions s/he typically can answer, then give feedback to the student in a neutral tone such as, "Today the straw doesn't seem to be helping your engine. Maybe try some chair push-ups instead of the straw to help your engine to get to just right."

**LOOKING FORWARD TO SINGING WITH YOU
AND YOUR STUDENTS THIS AFTERNOON!**

TEST DRIVE: Introducing the Alert Program® Through Song

JUST RIGHT SONG

```
    G                        D
Sometimes my engine runs high... woooo
    G                        D
Sometimes my engine runs... looooow
    G                        D    G
Sometimes my engine runs... Just Right!


          G                  D
There are things I can do to change my engine
G                    D
Put something in my mouth...
G               D
Take a big, deep breath... aaaaaahhhhhhhh,
G                            D    G
That can help my engine feel... Just Right!


          G                  D
There are things I can do to change my engine
G                    D
Move and push and pull... ugggggg.
G                        D
March and twiiiiiiiiiirl and jump, jump, jump, jump.
G                            D    G
That can help my engine feel... Just Right!
```

```
G                              D
Sometimes my engine runs high... woooo
G                              D
Sometimes my engine runs... looooow
G                          D   G
Sometimes my engine runs... Just Right!


            G                D
There are things I can use to change my engine
      G         D
A fidget in my hand...
      G           D
Brighten up my room...
      G          D
Listen to some tunes... hum, hum, hum.
G                          D   G
That can help my engine feel... Just Right!


G                              D
Sometimes my engine runs high... woooo
G                              D
Sometimes my engine runs... looooow
G                          D   G
Sometimes my engine runs... Just Right!


G                  D
What can I do to change my engine?
```

TEST DRIVE: Introducing the Alert Program® Through Song

```
G                        D
Put something in my mouth...
G                     D
Take a big, deep breath... aaaaaahhhhhhhh
G                      D
Move and push and pull... ugggggg.
G                          D
March and twiiiiiiiiiiiirl and jump, jump, jump, jump,
   G          D
A fidget in my hand...
    G           D
Brighten up my room...
     G          D
Listen to some tunes... hum, hum, hum...
G
That can make my engine feel...
D   G   D   G   D   G   D              G
Just right, Just Right, Just right, Juuuuuuuuuust Right!!!!
```

Lyrics: Elise Dirkse, Mary Sue Williams and Sherry Shellenberger

Music: L. Dennis Higgins and Dick Orr

Vocals: Sherry Shellenberger, Mary Sue Williams, and Mrs. Lethem's 4th & 5th Grade Zuni
Elementary School Class of 2005-2006

Musicians: L. Dennis Higgins and Dick Orr

BEST WORK

C
I do my best work and it's a great place to be,

When my engine's Just Right, there's nothin' stopping me.
E
So easy to find, more ways to show
C
All those around me, just what I know.
       G
Now, does my body, spend all day here?
        C
Nuh-uh. We all do things, to change our gear.

C
Amazing how low, my engine can go

When I'm feelin' brain dead, there's no one running the show.
F
My energy's going, down the drain
C
Simple school work, man, it feels like a pain.
    G
A jump start's needed, to get me in gear
       C
Or else doin' this work, could take all year!

TEST DRIVE: Introducing the Alert Program® Through Song

C

I do my best work and it's a great place to be,

When my engine's Just Right, there's nothin' stopping me.

F

So easy to find, more ways to show

C

All those around me, just what I know.

      G

Now, does my body, spend all day here?

       C

Nuh-uh. We all do things, to change our gear.

F

Downside of my engine, being on high

        C

Well it's makin' it tough for me to just get by.

F

Plenty of speed, but it's the antsy kind

    G

If I need to focus, I'm in a bind.

       F

To change my engine (to change my engine),

C

I know what it takes (I know what it takes)

F

Won't catch me makin', (Won't catch me makin'),

G
Won't catch me makin', no engine mistakes.

C
'Cause, I do my best work and it's a great place to be,

When my engine's Just Right, there's nothin' stopping me.
F
So easy to find, more ways to show
C
All those around me, just what I know.
G
Now, does my body, spend all day here?
C
Nuh-uh. We all do things, to change our gear.

Lyrics: Sherry Shellenberger and Don Wierman

Music: Don Wierman, L. Dennis Higgins, and Dick Orr

Vocals: Sherry Shellenberger and Mary Sue Williams

Musicians: L. Dennis Higgins, Dick Orr, and Don Wierman

TEST DRIVE: Introducing the Alert Program® Through Song

FIVE WAYS

```
G                            Am7
Five ways, we've got five ways
       D          G
To maximize your days.
G       G7    C    Cm    D
Mouth, Move, Touch, Look, Listen
                  G
And find your way.
```

```
          C
In your mouth there's much to do:
G
Bite, crunch, lick, blow, chew.
A                 A7
Engine changers can be dicey
        D
If you like it sweet, or sour, or spicy.
```

```
G                            Am7
Five ways, we've got five ways
       D          G
To maximize your days.
G       G7    C    Cm    D
Mouth, Move, Touch, Look, Listen
                  G
And find your way.
```

```
          C
On the move, or on the go
      G
No matter how fast or slow.
A                     A7
Front, back, circles, up or down
                D
When your body craves it, just move around.
          C
Heavy work is good for all
          G
If your engine starts to stall.
          A                     A7
If you find you're pumped or in a slump
D
It's OK to crash and bump.


G                             Am7
Five ways, we've got five ways
        D             G
To maximize your days.
G       G7    C     Cm    D
Mouth, Move, Touch, Look, Listen
                G
And find your way.
```

TEST DRIVE: Introducing the Alert Program® Through Song

```
        C
Touch is where some say
G
Fidgeting's now OK.
A
Click and tap and wiggle your pen
        D
How good it feels when the rhythm kicks in.


G                        Am7
Five ways, we've got five ways
       D           G
To maximize your days.
G     G7    C    Cm    D
Mouth, Move, Touch, Look, Listen
                     G
And find your way.


        C
With windows open wide
        G
And all the shades drawn high.
             A
When warm sunlight comes rushing in
             D
It'll change that frown into a grin.
```

```
G                              Am7
Five ways, we've got five ways
         D          G
To maximize your days.
G       G7    C    Cm    D
Mouth, Move, Touch, Look, Listen
                 G
And find your way.


      C
If irritating sounds
G
Slow your progress down.
      A
A squeaky chair, a dog that's barking
D
Time to get that engine sparking.
         C
With music that calms your soul
G
Classic or rock and roll.
        A
While some prefer to keep it quiet
D
Whatever it takes, make sure you try it!
```

TEST DRIVE: Introducing the Alert Program® Through Song

```
        G                    Am7
Five ways, we've got five ways
        D           G
To maximize your days.
G       G7    C    Cm    D
Mouth, Move, Touch, Look, Listen
                    G
And find your way.


        G                    Am7
Five ways, we've got five ways
        D           G
To maximize your days.
G             D       G
Five ways, we've got five ways!
```

Lyrics: Sherry Shellenberger and Don Wierman

Music: L. Dennis Higgins, Dick Orr, and Don Wierman

Vocals: Sherry Shellenberger and Mary Sue Williams

Musicians: L. Dennis Higgins, Dick Orr, and Don Wierman

ENGINE SONG

```
D              A
Stop, think, what's my plan?
                          D
Make a good decision, yes I can.
D              D7        G            G#dim
I can run my engine on a speed that's just right.
A                    D
Stop, think, what's my plan?


              D                        A
When I'm racing or cheering, jumping high in the sky,
                          D
Anyone can tell that my engine's on high.
                          D7
I take quick breaths, my heart pumps fast,
  G                G#dim  Bdim  Ddim  Fdim
I feel like I might never last.


What do you do?
A
Take a break (take a break)
A
Slow it down (slow it down)
A
Before I crash (before I crash)
```

TEST DRIVE: Introducing the Alert Program® Through Song

A
Into the ground (into the ground).

D   A
Stop, think, what's my plan?

                      D
Make a good decision, yes I can.

D   D7   G   G#dim
I can run my engine on a speed that's just right.

A   D
Stop, think, what's my plan?

          D
When I'm bored or feeling down,

     A
I just mope and frown.

My engine's on low,

   D
No energy head to toe.

 D
My heart lubs slow,

D7
I've got no go,

G
Can't hardly move,

       G#dim Bdim Ddim Fdim
No tae-kwon-do.

What do you do?

A

Call a friend (call a friend)

A

Hug a pet (hug a pet)

A

Munch a pickle (munch a pickle)

A

Don't forget (don't forget).

D   A

Stop, think, what's my plan?

                      D

Make a good decision, yes I can.

D   D7   G   G#dim

I can run my engine on a speed that's just right.

A   D

Stop, think, what's my plan?

D

Playing fair with my friends,

        A

Working hard at school,

Helping with a problem,

D

Keeping my cool.

D   D7

I'm in charge of my engine speed.

TEST DRIVE: Introducing the Alert Program® Through Song

```
G                       G#dim  Bdim  Ddim  Fdim
Just right speed I'll go indeed.


How does it feel?
A
Feels good inside (good inside)
A
Filled with pride (filled with pride)
A
Friends and family (friends and family)
A
Side by side (side by side).
D                          A
Stop, think, what's my plan?
                              D
Make a good decision, yes I can.
D                D7          G              G#dim
I can run my engine on a speed that's just right.
A                       D
Stop, think, what's my plan?
D                    D7          G          G#dim
Yes, I can run my engine on a speed that's just right.
A                        D      A D
Stop, think, what's my plan?
```

Lyrics: George Bednarczyk

Music: George Bednarczyk

Vocals: George Bednarczyk, Ms. Rosenberg's and Ms. Hoppenheit's
Margaret Peak School Classes of 2003-2004

Musicians: George Bednarczyk, Dan Donahue

ALIVE, AWAKE, ALERT

(Sung to *If You're Happy and You Know It* with motions similar to Head, Shoulders, Knees and Toes)

      A

I'm Alive, [touch toes]

Awake, [touch knees]

Alert, [touch shoulders]

   E

Enthusiastic [arms spread wide reaching for the sky]

      E

I'm Alive, [touch toes]

Awake, [touch knees]

Alert, [touch shoulders]

   A

Enthusiastic [arms spread wide reaching for the sky]

    D

Alive, [touch toes]

Awake, [touch knees]

Alert, [touch shoulders]

TEST DRIVE: Introducing the Alert Program® Through Song

A
Alert, [touch shoulders]

Awake, [touch knees]

Alive, [touch toes]

E
Alive, [touch toes]

Awake, [touch knees]

Alert, [touch shoulders]
A
Enthusiastic [arms spread wide reaching for the sky]

Music and lyrics: Public Domain

Vocals: Mary Sue Williams

Heckler: Sherry Shellenberger

Musician: Dick Orr

ISBN 0-9643041-3-9

90000